Coaching for Educators

Coaching for Educators

How to transform CPD in your school

Duncan Partridge

Open University Press

Open University Press
McGraw Hill
Unit 4,
Foundation Park
Roxborough Way
Maidenhead
SL6 3UD

email: emea_uk_ireland@mheducation.com
world wide web: www.openup.co.uk

First edition published 2022

A catalogue record of this book is available from the British Library

ISBN-13: 9780335251582
ISBN-10: 0335251587
eISBN: 9780335251599

Library of Congress Cataloging-in-Publication Data
CIP data applied for

Typeset by Transforma Pvt. Ltd., Chennai, India

Praise page

I've been convinced for some time now that coaching offers teachers and schools the means by which evidence from research into practice of what works well can be transferred back into practice, with impact. Too often, CPD engages teachers at an intellectual level but fails to transfer sufficiently back into the classroom. It skims across the surface of teachers' daily lives but doesn't penetrate fully into sustained change.

In 'Coaching for Educators', Duncan Partridge sets out with clarity why coaching can reach the parts that other kinds of CPD can't. The book contains a breadth of reference to other coaching literature, from education but also other walks of professional life, and locates the key insights and approaches firmly in educational settings.

Different coaching models are explained and the similarities and differences they offer demonstrated. I particularly valued the chapter on 'Coaching and the Brain' which illuminates how the 'deliberate practice' that effective coaching encourages can work powerfully on teachers' procedural knowledge. Coaching offers 'a formalised space for recall and reflection' so that change happens not because of actions you take, but because you are required to 'think about the doing'.

At the heart of the book's argument is the view of coaching as an approach that encourages professional conversations, structured through a number of possible 'dialogic models' which enable coach and 'coachee' to explore possibilities and reflections together. Coaching gets into the DNA of teaching – the embedded, often unconscious, engrained habits of a teaching career – and opens these up for thoughtful scrutiny.

As an authoritative, accessible digest of the 'why' and 'how' of coaching that acknowledges the messiness and complexity of the business of education, 'Coaching for Education' clears a lot of the undergrowth that can make coaching sometimes seem a bit impenetrable except to the already initiated and is a welcome addition to the literature of coaching and mentoring.

Alan Howe; By-Fellow, Hughes Hall, Cambridge University;
Associate, Oracy Cambridge

Contents

Acknowledgements

The list of people who have inspired and influenced the content of this book is far too long to include here, but I am grateful to them all for their guidance and wisdom.

I would like to specifically thank Paul Bennett and Howick College for allowing me to include their coaching story here and for giving up time to facilitate this.

Also, to my wife, Sarah, and sons, Louis and Max, just for being who they are.

Introduction

This book sets out to make the case for a coaching approach to professional development for teachers and school leaders. Drawing on research findings and real-life examples, it also aims to provide guidance and inspiration for the creation of cultures of coaching in schools. The hope is that the reader will finish the book with an understanding of differing dimensions of coaching in schools, insight into the impact such an approach can generate, as well as ideas and an enthusiasm for embedding coaching-based professional development in their own settings.

But before getting under the bonnet of coaching in schools, let's set the scene by taking a look at how professional development has typically happened in schools in the period since I started teaching, over 35 years ago, as well as some challenges associated with this.

My teaching career began in 1988 in a small, state-funded London primary school. There was a lot happening in English education at that time and it was an interesting and challenging period to join the profession. For one thing, a government-mandated National Curriculum had just been introduced, representing a big shift from the 'anything goes' system that existed previously. Bulky sets of colour-coded A4 ring binders containing new 'Programmes of Study' for each subject area were sent to us at regular intervals. As they arrived, my colleagues and I wrestled with their contents, coming to terms with the fact that we would no longer be able to teach whatever we wanted to teach, whenever we wanted to teach it, and the huge changes that this would herald for our classroom practice.

At the same time, 'Baker Days' for teachers were established. Jokes about cakes and bread for deserving teachers abounded, but rather than flour-based fun, these five days a year were introduced by the then Education Secretary, Kenneth Baker, to allow for 'professional learning' to take place. This represented a significant shift, as continuing professional development for teachers had previously been something of a hit or miss affair, with the extent to which this did or didn't happen being very much down to individual teachers and their schools. Now we had a government saying that ongoing development for teachers was so integral to system improvement, that it was mandating that at least 2.5 per cent of working days should be allocated for professional learning.

It is probably fair to say that in the early days, not every school made best use of the time that had been allocated. Indeed, in our school, once we'd used the first Baker Days to get our heads around the new National Curriculum, we struggled to figure out what to do with this suddenly conjured-up professional development time. Government guidance was sparse, so we ended up winging it a lot of the time. I remember a session where we learned new songs to teach the children in assembly, another was used for a potted history of the church the school was attached to, there was even a workshop where we tried out different types of paint for use in art lessons!

Baker Days, or INSET Days as they became known, have come a long way since then and are now part of a grand panoply of continuing professional development opportunities for UK teachers, which are usually firmly grounded in pedagogy and research-informed practice. Indeed, governments around the world are increasingly highlighting the importance of ongoing teacher education in improving systems and driving up standards. One international survey has determined that 63 per cent of all OECD member countries have compulsory CPD requirements for every teacher. The same report identified the most common forms of professional development that teachers experience as being: attending courses and seminars in person; reading professional literature; attendance at education conferences and online courses and seminars (OECD, 2019).

However, despite this global emphasis on CPD for education professionals, there are four fundamental challenges which I believe may be limiting the impact of all this in-service learning:

1 High quality CPD is costly and funds are scarce.
2 High quality CPD requires an investment of time, and due to the pressures of delivering curriculum content, accountability requirements and other factors, schools lack this time.
3 The pace of change in policies for schools, mandated by government, local authority or trusts, as well as our rapidly evolving understanding of 'what works' in the classroom may be creating a situation of 'initiative overload'.
4 Teachers can quickly form habits, which become deeply engrained and, therefore, professional development has limited impact.

High quality CPD is costly and funds are scarce

Research indicates that in recent years government spending on education in countries around the world has been in decline. Data shows that education funding fell from an average of 4.3 per cent of GDP in 2018 to 3.7 per cent of GDP in 2019 (World Bank, 2020). This trend has placed increasing financial pressures on state-funded schools and resulted in cost-cutting initiatives. In order to do this, many institutions are turning to what may be seen as the 'low hanging fruit' of CPD budgets. It would seem that, as this is an area of spending that can be perceived as not directly impacting students, it is easier for schools to justify reducing budgets in CPD than in other areas. Indeed, UK research shows that between 2018 and 2019, school spending on staff development declined by 8 per cent (School Dash, 2020).

Investment of time

High quality CPD requires an investment of time and, due to the pressures of delivering curriculum content, accountability requirements and other factors, schools lack this time. In an international report on *Teachers and School Leaders as Lifelong Learners* (OECD, 2019), a high percentage of teachers and leaders identified conflicting priorities and scheduling difficulties as a concrete barrier to participation in professional development activities. This trend was further illustrated in a UK survey of teachers which identified that increased workload around administrative tasks, student supervision, provision of evidence for the senior leadership team (SLT) and OFSTED, and changes to the curriculum had impacted the time and energy teachers had to engage in CPD opportunities (Scomis, 2017).

Initiative overload

The pace of change in policies for schools, mandated by government, local authority or trusts, as well as our rapidly evolving understanding of 'what works' in the classroom may be creating a situation of 'initiative overload'.

Education and our approach to schooling have always been subject to change, but the rate of this change over the last 20 years is maybe as rapid as it has ever been. The interplay between an increasingly sophisticated approach to educational research; the internet's democratisation of access to, and involvement in, this research; along with rapidly shifting and increasing levels of government involvement in what happens in the classroom, have led to a situation of 'initiative overload' (National Centre for Social Research for

CUBeC, 2012). This problem is characterised by schools, governments and other bodies piling schemes on top of one another, often in response to the latest 'trendy' thing in education, and not thinking through the implementation process sufficiently. When all this is combined with increasing workload and pressures in other areas, it is little wonder that teachers are left feeling overwhelmed, and record numbers are considering leaving the profession (Education Policy Institute, 2021a).

Habits

Teachers can quickly form habits, which become engrained, and therefore professional development has limited impact. The influential academic Dylan Wiliam famously said, 'Every teacher needs to improve, not because they are not good enough, but because they can be even better' (Wiliam, 2019). Wiliam was emphasising the importance of teachers guarding against professional stagnation and continuing to hone their skills throughout their career. It would seem, however, that this ongoing focus on improvement is not commonplace in teachers. Research indicates that after a period of rapid development at the start of a career in the classroom, teacher improvement tends to level off thereafter. This has been explained by the notion that in the early years of their career, teachers are getting to grips with the basics of their craft and making necessary adjustments to help them develop ways of working and routines that enable them to 'get by'. Once this state of 'basic competence' has been achieved, the approaches and strategies that got them there can become engrained as habitual practice. This habit formation can be understood through the neuroscientific theory that the repetition of patterns of thinking and behaviours leads to the creation of stronger and stronger neural pathways which guide action, and this in turn leads to automaticity of that action (Hobbis et al., 2021). This, of course, has implications for teachers' involvement in CPD. If by their third or fourth year in the classroom, teachers tend to have plateaued in their development and become habitual in their ways of working, it is less likely that any number of training sessions or workshops will result in meaningful change in practice.

In addition to these four challenges which can limit the impact of teacher CPD, it is also important to note that many teachers have expressed doubts about the actual quality of the professional development they have received. Teacher Tapp, a polling app for education professionals, found that less than a third of teachers agreed with the statement 'Time and resources allocated to professional development are used in ways that enhance teachers' instructional capabilities', with 40 per cent saying that their experience of CPD had had little or no effect on what they do in the classroom (Allen, 2019).

So, as well as contextual factors that can limit the impact of CPD for teachers, it seems there is a problem with the way we design and deliver professional development programmes. Chapter 3 of this book looks in detail at the factors that can make professional development effective or ineffective, but for the purposes of this Introduction, it is useful to highlight immediately the UK Department for Education's Standard for Teachers' Professional Development, which drew on international research findings to ascertain that effective CPD should do the following:

- be focused on 'improving and evaluating pupil outcomes';
- 'be underpinned by robust evidence and expertise';
- 'include collaboration and expert challenge';
- 'be sustained over time';
- 'be prioritised by school leadership'.

(Department for Education, 2016)

Despite an increasing prevalence of this type of guidance, teacher feedback would suggest that many school CPD programmes are still falling short of what is seen as best practice.

I would suggest that if we are to improve the impact of teacher development, and, at the same time, boost the effect that this has on pupil outcomes, we need to think about how we can implement a system which has the following characteristics:

1 It is cost-effective.
2 It is time-efficient and manageable.
3 It is focused and avoids potential for overload in teachers.
4 It takes into account the tendency for teachers to develop engrained habits.
5 It is in line with research-informed guidance on best practice.

This book makes the argument that a system of professional development for teachers, that focuses on coaching, has the potential to demonstrate all of these characteristics. As an approach that can be delivered flexibly and largely 'in house', there is scope for ensuring it is both cost-effective and manageable. Similarly, being focused, incremental and goal-oriented in nature, coaching offers professional learning which is personalised and designed to help teachers practise new ways of working and thinking. And, finally, there is plentiful evidence that coaching in schools works, and when the approach is assessed against the criteria of the UK Standard for Professional Development outlined above, coaching can certainly be said to be 'focused on improving and evaluating pupil outcomes'; to be 'underpinned by robust evidence and expertise'; to 'include collaboration and expert challenge'; to be 'sustained over time'; and one would hope that the case made here would lead to it being 'prioritised by school leadership'.

The structure of the book

To conclude this Introduction, I have included a brief bullet-pointed outline of each chapter. Although each part of the book builds on the last, chapters can also be dipped into and read in isolation, and I hope the reader will find these summaries useful in guiding them through the areas being explored, and pointing them to those of particular interest or pertinence in their work at any moment in time.

Chapter 1 What is coaching?

- The origins of coaching in sport and business contexts
- The purpose and nature of coaching conversations
- Attributes and attitudes which underpin coaching
- The GROW coaching model

Chapter 2 Dimensions of coaching in schools

- How coaching can help schools achieve their priorities
- Clearing up misconceptions
- Differing approaches to coaching in schools
- School-focused coaching models compared and contrasted

Chapter 3 The case for coaching as professional development

- What does effective professional development for teachers look like and how does coaching link with this?
- Research evidence for the impact of a coaching approach in schools

Chapter 4 Coaching and wellbeing

- Exploring current concerns about mental health and wellbeing in schools
- Coaching, Positive Psychology and Growth Mindset
- Addressing self-limiting beliefs through coaching

Chapter 5 Coaching and the brain

- Understanding how the delivery and impact of coaching link to cognitive science

Chapter 6 Building and sustaining a culture of coaching

- Essential elements for successfully building and sustaining a culture of coaching
- Understanding and managing the process of change involved in building and sustaining a culture of coaching

Chapter 7 Howick College: placing coaching at the heart of professional learning

- A case study of Howick College in New Zealand, where a coaching approach to professional development has been embedded across the school

1 What is coaching?

There are many different definitions of coaching. Some of these appear contradictory of each other and others could be accused of a certain 'New Age' vagueness. I have developed my own definition, which is born out of my studies and experience in the field. I make no claim to definitiveness, but it is the definition which underpins the content of this book.

> Coaching can be described as facilitated self-learning, usually involving a series of one-to-one conversations, where powerful questions, listening which seeks to understand, appropriate challenge, and occasionally proffered advice are carefully deployed by the coach to support a coachee to identify and work towards goals in a practical, positive and optimistic manner.

However, this notion of coaching may not be the one that springs to mind for many people when the word is mentioned. Rather, it may well conjure up an image of a sports coach, baseball hat on head, whistle round neck, pointing in all directions and barking out instructions. And, as it happens, coaching, in its business and education setting sense, did indeed grow out of sports coaching.

In 1974, Timothy Gallwey published his book, *The Inner Game of Tennis*, in which he suggested that a player needs to address an inner struggle against doubts, fears and self-limiting beliefs, as much as they need to focus on outwitting or outhitting their opponent. Gallwey later built on his thinking about the inner game and presented it as a formula:

$P = p - i$ (Performance = potential − interference).

Gallwey suggested that rather than just teaching techniques, a tennis coach should also ask questions and give instructions which allow a player to focus on reducing interference, whether this is related to self-limiting beliefs or to what is happening with the ball, the racket or their own body. Gallwey's coaching approach thus evolved towards inviting his coachees to identify goals they would like to achieve (for example, to improve their volleying), before then asking awareness-raising questions which resulted in the player identifying what they needed to do to improve (for example, what do you notice about how you are holding the racket when the ball goes in the net and how you are holding the racket when the ball goes over the net?) (ibid.).

Gallwey's revolutionary ideas about sports coaching were picked up on in the late 1970s by John Whitmore and Graham Alexander, who, having initially used the approach with skiers, started to believe coaching had relevance to the business community. Together Whitmore and Alexander coined the term Performance Coaching, and took Gallwey's idea of using questioning and awareness-raising to improve performance, to work with business leaders, helping them apply this in development conversations with team-members instead of the typically top-down 'I tell – you do' interactions that had tended to dominate previously (Whitmore, 2017). In Whitmore's own words, coaching was 'helping them to learn rather than teaching them' (ibid., p. 13).

In order to scaffold and structure coaching conversations which are productive and focused, Whitmore developed a framework, providing distinct stages to the questioning involved in the process: the GROW (Goal, Reality, Options, Will) model.

GROW was the first coaching framework, and is still probably the most commonly used model, having been used over the years to guide many coaching conversations in differing contexts (we will explore GROW in greater detail along with other coaching frameworks later in this chapter). However, Whitmore's seminal influence on the development of coaching extends beyond GROW; his work was also very important in building our understanding of the qualities and skills coaches need in order to have a genuine impact.

Coaching skills and qualities: emotional intelligence

Whitmore stresses that coaching is much more than the sum of its parts: 'It is a way of leading and managing, a way of treating people, a way of thinking, a way of being' (Whitmore, 2017, p. 39).

Whitmore's work on coaching bears close relation to the theory of emotional intelligence (EI), which suggests that, as a counterpart to cognitive intelligence, we have varying abilities to understand feelings, goals, intentions, responses and behaviour, both in ourselves and others (Goleman, 1995). Coaching can be seen as a process that raises a coachee's awareness of their EI, fosters insight into how this supports or limits their ability to achieve their goals, and supports development in this area. At the same time a coach's engagement in the process can in itself be understood as a practical manifestation of emotional intelligence; a coach who is not modelling or seeking to develop their own EI is not authentically or effectively engaging in the process and therefore undermining its impact.

Five domains of EI have been identified: (1) self-awareness; (2) self-regulation; (3) motivation; (4) empathy; and (5) social skills (ibid.). We will take each of these in turn and explore how they relate to coaching.

Self-awareness in coaching

One of the fundamental purposes of a coaching conversation is to help raise a coachee's awareness of the emotional factors that are helping or hindering them in trying to achieve something or reach a goal. The judicious use of questioning (see p. 14) and appropriate challenge helps a coachee develop the self-awareness to recognise emotions, habits and triggers, and the impact they have in enabling or restricting them in moving towards their goals. A coach who has a high level of self-awareness will model this in their interactions and also use it to help them guide conversations and ask questions which are useful for the coachee.

Self-regulation in coaching

Self-regulation can be understood as an ability to manage one's emotions appropriately, as well as to hold oneself to account for one's actions or inaction. Effective coaching helps a coachee to take responsibility for working towards their goals. To do this, a coach does not hold a coachee to account themselves, rather they support a coachee so that they are able to move towards holding themselves to account. As with self-awareness, self-regulation should be both modelled by a coach and used to shape the approach they take in their coaching.

Motivation in coaching

An important part of the coach's role is to help the coachee tune in to the drivers and values that underpin their goals. Raising awareness in these areas helps the coachee become more motivated to carry out planned actions and work towards their aim, as they are more able to explicitly link their plans and actions to their fundamental belief systems.

Empathy in coaching

As well focusing on raising awareness of one's own emotions and the impact these have on how we behave, coaching also provides a space for reflecting on and understanding the emotions of others and how they relate to the areas being explored and goals that are established. Clearly, a coach will also need to adopt an empathetic approach in their work; tuning into the emotions and responses of the coachee plays a crucial role in enabling the conversation to be developed and guided in a helpful and sensitive way.

Social skills in coaching

Rapport between a coach and a coachee is very important. The state of feeling relaxed with and responsive to another person is a precondition for any productive coaching conversation. On the part of the coach, this means demonstrating a genuine interest in the coachee and the area they wish to focus on. On the part of the coachee, this means a willingness to be open and to think deeply. Of course, underpinning rapport, there needs to be a relationship of genuine trust between coach and coachee. Respecting confidentiality, avoiding unpredictable behaviour and respecting agreements are all important in developing an effective coaching relationship. In order to ensure these are all in place, the process of *contracting* is often seen as a crucial element of coaching practice. Contracting essentially consists of agreement setting before a session or series of sessions, thereby creating a context of predictability and the establishment of boundaries for the work to be done. Areas covered in the contracting process may include: confidentiality, responsibilities, commitment to honesty, areas not to be discussed and anything else that a coachee or coach may feel is necessary to agree in order to create a trusting and productive coaching relationship.

Coaching skills and qualities: listening (to the coachee and to your intuition)

In one of the most successful books on business ever published, *The 7 Habits of Highly Effective People* (Covey, 1989), habit number 5 is centred on empathetic communication. The book posits that the reality is that 'most people do not listen with the intent to understand; they listen with the intent to reply' (ibid., p. 264) and that a deep shift in paradigm is needed for conversations to move beyond being 'collective monologues' (ibid., p. 265).

My own experience over the years has been that effective listening is indeed a very difficult skill to master. When engaging in a conversation, all too often the words I am hearing from the other party play into a personal narrative in my head, and I use them to advance my own agenda, picking up on points that help take the discussion in the direction I want it to. My training as a coach required me to work hard to lose this habit. The coach's role in a pure coaching conversation involves setting aside judgement and personal views, and the adoption of a neutral position where the only agenda is the coachee's agenda. In short, the conversational space needs to 'belong to' the coachee, with the coach taking the role of 'thought partner' and facilitator, rather than being a protagonist in the dialogue.

There are various strategies that a coach can draw on in order to ensure they are listening effectively and communicating this to the coachee. A fairly obvious one is connected to body language; clearly eye contact, nodding and an open stance says 'I'm listening' much more effectively than an averted gaze and folded arms. However, as anybody who has ever taught a class of children whose outward appearance leads one to believe they are tuned in to every word, only to find out later that this certainly wasn't the case, body language is not always a good proxy for effective listening.

Table 1.1 outlines some other strategies that may be deployed by a coach in the name of effective listening, and the impact that these generate.

It should also be noted that, as well as generating the impacts described above, all of these strategies should have the effect of making the coachee feel listened to. This is really important in fostering the trust and rapport that must exist between a coach and coachee in an effective relationship.

A skilled coach will be able to deploy all of these strategies in an intentional way, as they support a coachee in exploring their situation and planning to move forward. Although the strategies are not presented here as a hierarchy, it could be argued that as one moves through Table 1.1, the strategies become less pragmatic and more illustrative of a nuanced high quality coaching relationship. Certainly, a coach's ability to decide when it would be useful for them to share their 'wonderings' is a sophisticated skill. Similarly, a strategically deployed silence may prompt a coachee to access insights and ideas, in a way which would not be possible were such a conversational space not provided.

Perhaps the most impactful of all these strategies/skills, and worthy of further exploration, is that of intuiting. Intuition in coaching is the ability to gain insight into something significant which

Table 1.1   Effective listening strategies

Strategy/Skill	Description	Impact
Summarising	Highlighting main points	Gives coachee an opportunity to reflect on what they have said
Clarifying	Checking understanding	Reduces possibility of misunderstanding or miscommunication
Reflecting	Repeating exact words back	Highlights something of potential importance that has been said
Wondering	Sharing an idea or insight that has been prompted by what was said	Demonstrates to coachee that their words have generated a thought process
Silence	Letting coachee's words 'hang in the air'	Powerful way of providing space for further reflection at a significant moment
Intuiting	Reading between the words and tuning into something of potential significance	Takes session onto a new level, possibly providing platform for a breakthrough moment

goes beyond the actual words being uttered. As something which is automatic and unconscious, intuition can be perceived as being almost magical but in fact it is a cognitive process. Psychologists believe that intuition is rooted in the brain's tendency to try and make sense of something being experienced by combing the long-term memory for similar experiences, and then pattern matching (*Psychology Today*, 2021). The concept of System 1 and System 2 thinking (Kahneman, 2011) provides us with further insight into the nature of intuition. Whereas System 2 thinking is connected to slow deliberative decision-making, intuition can be seen as part of System 1 thinking, which is fast and instinctive. Kahneman argues that our intuitive System 1 thinking is more likely to be correct if: (1) it relates to predictable, non-complex situations; (2) it draws on a large sample size of previous experiences; and (3) immediate and accurate feedback is received.

What does this mean for coaching practice? I would suggest Kahneman's work has the following implications:

1   A coach needs to be aware of their intuition as a cognitive process and be willing to tune in to their System 1 thinking.

2   The wider a coach's experience in the field of coaching, and in relevant professional contexts, the larger the 'database' of experiences the brain draws on in generating an intuitive response, and therefore the more likely an insight is to be accurate.

3   A coach should seek feedback from a coachee as to the accuracy or pertinence of an intuition: 'I am sensing that maybe … does that resonate at all?'

4   An important part of intuition is 'social' in nature and linked to non-verbal cues; these can provide insight into how a coachee is feeling or experiencing a situation. Coaches should therefore practise paying attention to these.

5   Intuition is not always correct. It is prone to errors and cognitive biases. Coaches should be mindful of this and not always 'trust their gut'.

Coaching skills and qualities: questioning

Questioning is probably the most important tool a coach has in their armoury. As John Whitmore put it, a coach's 'powerful questions' 'focus attention and evoke clarity … increase coachees' self-belief and self-motivation … help coachees learn, grow and achieve success' (2017, p. 83).

Coaching frameworks often have 'suggested questions' associated with each stage of the process. Less experienced coaches who are developing their confidence in the approach may particularly benefit from the scaffolded structure such models offer. However, coaches who have developed a level of expertise will tend to avoid referring to lists of questions, as an over-use of these can feel artificial and impede a session's natural flow. Ideally coaches should draw on the listening skills outlined above to ensure that their line of questioning is truly responsive to what is being said and framed by the emerging insights of the coachee.

Although it is not possible to define precisely what the qualities of a good coaching question are, there are certain characteristics which most questions share that are useful to the process of moving a coachee forward. Powerful coaching questions are: concise and comprehensible; positively pitched; usually open; attuned to the coachee's, not the coach's, agenda; persistent in nature; and aha-moment-inducing.

Concise and comprehensible questions

Ideally, during a session, a coachee will quickly find themselves in a space of deep personal reflection, where their cognitive resources are focused on digging deep to find insights, answers and wells of resources that they can draw on to move forward. In this state, they will not benefit from complex, drawn-out, multi-part questions, which sap their cognitive energies as they try to understand what is being asked of them. Simplicity is key to effective questioning in coaching.

Positively pitched questions

One part of the definition of coaching being used in this book states that the process should help the coachee 'identify and work towards goals in a practical, positive and optimistic manner'. In line with this, a coach should avoid questions which allow the coachee to spend too much time focusing on 'what is going wrong'. Although it is certainly good practice to explore the coachee's current situation and how it is impacting on where they want to get to, an over-emphasis on problems can end up being counterproductive.

Similarly, it is important to avoid questions that may elicit a defensive response. It is all too easy for a well-intentioned question to be taken in the wrong way. 'Why' questions, particularly, can be problematic. A question as simple as *'Why did you do it that way?'* runs the risk of being interpreted as an implied criticism. Much better to reframe such a question along the lines of, 'Can you talk me through the decision-making process that led you to do it in this way?' This may seem like a minor point but when we remember the importance of trust and rapport in a coaching relationship, it is vital that coaches are mindful of the language they use, so that potential misinterpretations are avoided wherever possible.

Usually open questions

As every teacher knows, closed questions, usually requiring a simple yes or no answer, are not useful for opening up discussions. On the other hand, carefully crafted open questions can lead to rich dialogue. The same holds true in coaching conversations. Consider these two coaching questions, which may typically be asked after a coachee has decided on a course of action:

1 Are you committed to following through on your plan?
2 What things may hold you back on following through on your plan?

Whereas the former would normally elicit a simple 'yes' or 'no', or possibly a 'maybe', the latter requires the coachee to deepen their level of commitment by pro-actively thinking about (and therefore planning to offset) potential obstacles.

It is important to stress here that although open questions should probably be regarded as a default setting for coaches, there will be times when a closed question may be useful in furthering a session, often in a specific, practical sense. Some examples are: checking the coach has understood something correctly ('Am I correct in saying that …?'); asking for permission to offer advice ('May I make a suggestion?'); and inquiring as to the utility of a line of discussion ('Is this useful for you?').

Questions attuned to the coachee's, not the coach's, agenda

A common mistake coaches make is to ask questions in such a way as to 'lead' coachees towards a solution or idea they already have in mind. This is clearly not in the spirt of coaching as 'facilitated self-learning'. Simply asking questions is not coaching, rather, coaches should seek to ask questions in an open-minded way, thereby generating a process of joint inquiry. It may well be that at some stage, a coach senses that it is appropriate to suggest a course of action to a coachee. This is entirely appropriate (as long as it does not become the default approach), especially if the coachee is given the option of accepting or not accepting the offered advice. Certainly this is a preferential course of action to 'pretending' to coach by asking leading questions.

Persistent questions

Coaching is neither a superficial nor a rapid process. Coachees need time to think deeply about the areas they are focusing on, and coaches need to be patient and persistent in their approach to facilitating this. This will mean that elements of the questioning process may sometimes feel uncomfortably drawn-out. Coaching aims to get to the root of issues and to provide a space for in-depth exploration of solutions. To bring this about, a coach may need to pursue a line of questioning for some time, in order to help the coachee really get to the nub of something that is going on for them. Similarly, when coming up with possible solutions and strategies, my experience has shown me that it is often only at the end of a very long series of 'and what else could you do?' type questions that a coachee arrives at an idea that really works for them. Drawn-out thoughtful silences can be part of this process. Coaches should resist the temptation to jump in and fill the gap in these situations, as this is often 'where the magic happens'.

Aha-moment-inducing questions

These types of questions are, by nature, esoteric, and it is tempting to define them by stating 'you'll know one when you've asked one'. However, an anecdote from my own coaching work is probably a better way to illustrate aha-moment-inducing questions and how they can come about.

This exchange took place in the course of working with an international school middle leader, who had aspirations to senior leadership and had engaged my services to support him in working towards his goal. Having explored his current situation in some detail, it was becoming clear that he was seeking to move away from what he described as a 'low-profile and humble' approach that he felt was holding him back from developing professionally. I asked him what he thought it was about this approach that was leading to him being held back. In response, he paused for some time and then said: 'I suppose it means that people just don't notice what I contribute to the team.' I didn't respond immediately but when I did, it was to ask, 'How do you know that people don't notice what you contribute?' After some thought, he shook his head and said, 'I don't know … maybe because they don't tell me?' At this point, sensing a potentially important moment, I asked him, 'So if you were to *ask* your team what they felt were the most important qualities you bring to the work you do together, what do you think they would say?' He pondered, 'Um, maybe … authenticity … and …' at this point, he began to smile, 'I suppose humility, not making it all about me!' My coachee had come to a realisation that something he felt was holding him back was in fact probably an important element of what made him an effective middle leader.

There is nothing particularly significant or insightful in itself about the question, 'So if you were to ask your team what they felt were the most important qualities you bring to the work you do together, what do you think they would say?' In fact, it could even be argued that it is far too long and wordy to be a 'good' coaching question. However, it became an aha-moment-inducing question, because I was able to draw on an intuition (which in retrospect, I could see came from my experience and knowledge of what teams appreciate in leaders), to ask something that allowed my coachee to think differently about his approach and the impact it had on his team.

Coaching skills and qualities: use of metaphor

Metaphors are both hugely powerful in shaping how humans perceive the world, and surprisingly commonplace in our day-to-day communication. It has been estimated that in conversation we use metaphors, on average, six times per minute (Geary, 2009). By substituting one thing for another, metaphors tap into a seemingly natural tendency human beings have to understand through story and imagery. In fact, metaphors are so commonplace that often we don't even notice they are there. The phrases 'heart of stone', 'blood from a stone', and 'stony silence', for example, are immediately understood without conscious contemplation of rocks or boulders.

There is a coaching approach called Clean Language (Wilson, 2017), which explicitly places metaphor at the centre of its process, through 12 set questions which help a coachee understand, and when needed move beyond the personal metaphors that shape their understanding of a situation.

However, even when used in a less-structured way, metaphors can be very useful in helping coachees explore their circumstances and frame their goals. Either through working with a metaphor that a coachee introduces or by deploying a metaphor themselves in order to share their understanding of a coachee's situation, a coach can create a playing-field (see what I did there?) on which a coachee's aims and goals can be explored.

As an example, while working together with the coachee referred to in the anecdote above, we developed the metaphor of a 'shop window' where he could choose and display those elements of his experience and skill set that he wished his current and any potential employer to be aware of. With my prompting, he dressed and re-dressed his shop window, until he was happy that it represented him as a professional. Interestingly, he also later deployed the metaphor during what turned out to be a successful interview for a senior position.

Coaching skills and qualities: contracting

The final skill/quality covered in this section actually refers to something that should happen at the very start of a coaching relationship. As its name suggests, contracting involves agreeing the format and boundaries of a coaching relationship. By establishing what a coachee can expect from a coach, and vice versa, the process plays an important part in creating trust and transparency in the relationship. Contracting in coaching is usually carried out in the form of a set of verbal agreements, rather than through the production of a written document. Areas covered may include practical considerations, such as timings and locations, as well as factors related to the nature of the relationship, such as confidentiality, giving or receiving feedback and commitment to being open and honest. Clearly, once made, these agreements have to be stuck to, in order for the relationship to flourish. This is not to say contracts cannot be modified, as the sessions unfold and the relationship evolves, however, clarity and consistency should always characterise the nature of any agreements.

The difference between coaching and mentoring

The difference between coaching and mentoring can be an area of confusion, and this is not helped by the fact that the words are often used interchangeably.

As a reminder, the definition of coaching I use is as follows:

> Coaching can be described as facilitated self-learning, usually involving a series of one-to-one conversations, where powerful questions, listening which seeks to understand, appropriate challenge, and occasionally proffered advice are carefully deployed by the coach to support a coachee to identify and work towards goals in a practical, positive and optimistic manner.

Similarly, I have developed a definition of mentoring:

> Mentoring can be described as expert support, often but not solely, provided to professionals who are new in their roles, where the focus is on the offering of advice and sharing of knowledge.

For me and many other practitioners, coaching and mentoring sit at opposite ends of a spectrum. This implies that one can use a purely coaching approach or a purely mentoring approach to support a person's development but also that both approaches can be drawn on with differing levels of emphasis at different times. Moreover, a skilled practitioner will move along the continuum, varying the emphasis of their approach depending on the evolving needs and focus of the person being worked with.

The GROW coaching model

As already mentioned, GROW (**G**oal, **R**eality, **O**ptions, **W**ill), as developed by John Whitmore, was the first coaching framework. Since then, many other models, each with its own quirky mnemonic, have been developed. Among these are: OSKAR (**O**utcome, **S**caling, **K**now-how, **A**ffirm and **A**ctions, **R**eview), STEPPA (**S**ubject, **T**arget, **E**motion, **P**erception, **P**lan, **P**ace, **A**ction) and CIGAR (**C**urrent **R**eality, **I**deal, **G**aps, **A**ction, **R**eview). However, these are all very much variations on GROW and Whitmore's model still remains probably the most commonly used. We will explore some models which were developed specifically for educational contexts in Chapter 2, but a more detailed breakdown of GROW will provide insight into how a framework can serve the purpose of scaffolding coaching conversations.

Whitmore was very careful to point out that GROW is not coaching in itself, merely a vehicle which is only effective when used 'in the context of awareness and responsibility and the intention and skill to generate them through active listening and powerful questions' (2017, p. 99). Whitmore also stressed that the model should be used flexibly, echoing the point made earlier about the pitfalls of sticking rigidly to a 'script' of coaching questions, thereby sacrificing the potential for responsiveness in the moment.

Goal-setting

Goal-setting is a complex area and many books have been written on this area alone. The most widely used approach employed to guide the setting of goals is probably the SMART method (**S**pecific, **M**easurable, **A**chievable, **R**ealistic, **T**ime-framed). This model certainly has some applicability when it comes to setting coaching goals. SMART provides a very good way of ensuring goals are tangible and practically deliverable. What SMART does lack, however, is an 'emotional' element, a quality which factors in motivation.

An alternative to SMART, which captures these missing elements, is the EXACT model (**E**xplicit, '**X**citing', **A**ssessable, **C**hallenging, **T**ime-framed) (Wilson, 2014). EXACT was developed specifically for use in coaching situations. It retains some of the pragmatism of SMART, but the inclusion of 'Xciting' and Challenging in the model implies that goals also need to be both inspiring and suitably stretching in order to be truly motivating for coachees.

A goal which is set at the start of a series of coaching sessions will thereafter be the lens through which everything is viewed as the process moves forward. Therefore, it is important that as well as being explicit, assessable, challenging and time-framed, the goal is framed by the kind of aspirational and inspirational language that can motivate and drive a coachee forward through the dips and challenges they will inevitably encounter. As an example, a goal like 'improve communication between the leadership team and staff' is perfectly functional, but it is neither particularly exciting nor motivating. On the other hand, if the goal can be reframed so that it captures the positive and motivating implications of it being achieved, it can take on a different quality. So, if 'improve communication between the leadership team and staff' is reframed along the lines of something like, 'everyone knows and everyone understands', the goal retains the same essence as the original but is now more like a mission or mantra for the coachee. A goal framed in this way can be drawn on as a kind of 'golden thread' through the whole coaching process, generating energy and enthusiasm along the way.

Here, are some sample coaching questions that could be used by a coach when supporting a coachee to identify an EXACT goal:

- What exactly do you want to achieve?
- How could you aim even higher?
- How can you reframe this to make the language more exciting and inspiring?
- How will you know you have achieved this?
- What evidence will you need?
- How will it feel when you achieve this?
- When do you want to have achieved this by?

It should be stressed that this list is neither definitive nor exhaustive. A line of questioning should ultimately be defined by what a coachee is saying, rather than a coach's checklist.

Reality

The Reality stage of GROW provides the coach with an opportunity to develop an understanding of their coachee's context and, more importantly, for the coachee to reflect deeply on their current situation and how it relates to their goal.

In a coaching context, this stage involves the coach using questioning to enable the coachee to develop awareness and insight into their current situation. It could be understood as a mini-SWOT analysis, where **S**trengths, **W**eaknesses, **O**pportunities and **T**hreats are considered and reflected on. The coach should encourage the coachee to focus on only current circumstances and not the past, adopting a neutral, exploratory approach to do so. This guards against energy-sapping negativity creeping in at this stage, and also reduces the likelihood of the conversation becoming focused on others or historical events, which may not be relevant and could stymie the process of self-reflection.

A coach will need to demonstrate authentic curiosity at this stage, not in a prying or intrusive sense, but in such a way that may help the coachee to gain perspectives they might not previously have been aware of. Listening skills are particularly important at this stage, as there is always a strong possibility that a coachee will say something significant that would benefit from further analysis and thought. Bringing these key moments to a coachee's attention is only possible if the coach is deeply engaged with the process and truly tuned in to the coachee, their words, as well as their physical demeanour.

Again, I will illustrate this with an anecdote, which relates to a coaching session I had with a headteacher of a privately owned international school. This coachee was having difficulties in her relationship with the school owner and had asked for coaching to help her improve this situation. While we were discussing a particularly challenging series of meetings that had taken place, I was struck by the strength of some of the language in her descriptions of what was going on in these meetings and decided to note down some of the words she was using. During a natural pause, I asked her if she minded me playing back to her some of the words she had used to describe the meetings. She agreed and I went through the list, which contained terms such as 'tense', 'rambling', 'superficial', 'one-sided' and 'insincere'. I then asked her, if she could choose just one, which of those things would she like to be different about the meetings and why? After some deliberation, she chose 'insincere', as this was at odds with the strong professional values she held . We then went on to discuss what sincerity actually looked like in meetings and other contexts. Having done this, we decided to revisit her goal, and built in the idea of sincerity so that it became a central theme in future coaching sessions. The noting of her words, and further exploration of what lay behind them, were key for the whole coaching process, as it captured the essence of what my coachee was finding challenging. Had I started the session with the question, 'What would you like to change about the meetings?', she might well not have given the same answer. The reality stage of the process had provided us with the opportunity to 'chew the cud' as to what was going on for this coachee. In my role as a coach, I was able to tune in to what she was saying and 'shine a light' on what appeared to me to be key phrases that warranted further exploration.

With the same caveats that were mentioned in relation to the questions listed in the Goal section, here are some sample Reality questions which may typically be used at this stage:

- What's happening for you at the moment?
- What have you done so far?
- What is really working in your favour here?
- What may be holding you back?
- What resources do you have at your disposal which may be useful?

It is very important to stress here that the Reality stage of GROW *does not equate to therapy*. Therapy is a healing process conducted by highly qualified practitioners and is focused on helping people understand how past experiences may be negatively impacting their current mental health. Coaching, by contrast, is goal-focused, and uses a consideration of the present in order to make plans for the future. This distinction should be made very clear to a coachee, ideally as part of the contracting process at the beginning of a coaching relationship. If at any stage a coachee discloses something which raises an alarm and goes beyond the normal parameters of a coaching conversation, or if a coachee shows any signs of significant distress or possible mental illness, a coach should point them towards a suitably qualified professional, rather than attempt to deal with the situation themselves.

Options

The Options stage of GROW is about exploring different actions and strategies that could be used by the coachee to move them towards their goal. Somewhat counter-intuitively, at this stage, the quantity of options probably trumps the quality of options. This is not to say that the aim is to focus on sub-optimal solutions, rather, that it is to explore all sorts of possible lines of action, including those that may at first appear undeliverable or impractical. It is important that the coachee does not hold back at this stage and to facilitate this, the coach should be persistent in eliciting as many options as possible, as well as deploying questions that encourage creative thinking which is not restricted by habitual thought patterns.

At this stage, a coach may also decide to offer a suggestion themselves. Ideally this should be a strategy that is used sparingly, once the coachee appears to have exhausted their own list of options, and proffered as another possibility, rather than imposed as a solution. As we know, the main function of a coach is to facilitate solution finding, rather than provide guidance. However, it would be doing a disservice to a coachee if a coach were to hold back an idea that may be useful.

Having been through this 'brainstorming' phase, it is often then useful for the coach to use questioning to help the coachee carry out a cost-benefit analysis of the options listed, the results of which should provide a neat segue into the final stage of GROW.

Sample options questions:

- What could you do to achieve your goal?
- What else?
- Anything else?
- Is there something else?
- Imagine (*a named barrier*) wasn't there, what could you do then?
- May I offer an idea at this stage?

Will

As the name suggests, Will, the final phase of GROW, is focused on making decisions as to which option(s) a coachee 'will' choose and put into action. An important characteristic of this stage is that it should be used to help the coachee build commitment to follow through on their plans. The coach seeks to support the coachee to be accountable for their actions (or inaction) but is not responsible for holding the coachee to account themselves.

A part of this process involves exploring and planning to overcome any obstacles that may be encountered. More important than this, though, is a focus on building personal responsibility and enthusiasm for the plan of action. The sample questions outlined below illustrate how the coach may facilitate this process. You will notice in the list, an example of a 'scaling question', where a coachee is asked to give a score to their level of commitment to action. These types of question, when used with follow-ups such as those listed below, can be particularly useful in facilitating reflection and also in generating determination to move forwards.

Sample will questions:

- Which of these options will best help you achieve your goal?
- When will you carry out these actions?
- How will it feel if you achieve your goal through carrying out these actions?
- What obstacles might hold you back from carrying out these actions?

- How can you overcome those obstacles?
- On a scale of 1–10 how likely are you to follow through on this plan?
- What could you do to make this score higher?

The rise of coaching

Coaching is increasingly prevalent in the corporate sector. It has been estimated that in the USA alone, the market size of the executive coaching industry in 2021 was US$ 10.9bn, with an annual growth rate of 5.8 per cent (IBIS World, 2021). From Fortune 500 companies, to small start-ups, investment in coaching is increasing, as companies seek to reap the benefits that access to internal or external coaches seems to offer them.

So, what are these benefits? One study (McGovern, 2001) used the results of a survey of different companies to estimate that on average they saw an ROI (return on investment) in coaching of nearly 600 per cent (in other words, every dollar spent on coaching resulted in 6 dollars of additional income for the company).

However, isolating the impact of coaching and attributing a monetary value to this is very difficult and is always likely to be prone to error. Given this, it is perhaps better to look at the results of qualitative surveys in order to gain insight into why companies are prepared to invest in coaching for their employees. A meta-analysis of the results of a number of studies looking at the impact of coaching in corporate settings reported that coaching had significantly positive effects on employee performance, mental health, coping attitudes and goal-directed self-regulation (Theeboom et al., 2014). These results, with their implications for both a business' profitability and for its employees' wellbeing, go some way to explaining the growth of coaching in the corporate sector. If we substitute student outcomes for profit, these categories are equally pertinent for the education sector. However, there are differences as well as similarities in how coaching is used in schools as compared to corporate settings and we now turn to exploring the dimensions of coaching in a school context.

2 Dimensions of coaching in schools

In his famous book, *The 7 Habits of Highly Effective People*, Stephen Covey (1989) defined the seventh habit as 'sharpening the saw', in other words, seeking out continuous improvement opportunities. Few would argue against the logic of this: after all, if we are always trying to get better at what we do, surely the outcomes can only be beneficial for everyone. But Covey also warned that it is easy to become so focused on doing the sawing, that one neglects to take the time to sharpen the blade. This is certainly a risk for people who work in schools. The demand and pressures of teaching are such that finding time and energy to devote to professional development activities is very difficult. Indeed, as well as finding the time for professional development, a lack of funds is often another barrier for schools when it comes to providing CPD opportunities for their teachers and leaders. Given the scarcity of these resources, it is particularly vital for schools to see a good return on the time and money they invest in professional development.

The metric used to measure ROI in CPD for businesses is usually monetary; in other words, for every unit of currency invested in employee development, how many additional units of currency are generated? Measuring ROI in CPD for schools, however, is much more complex. It is true to say that for many privately owned or run schools, generation of profit is an important aim, but even these settings will tend to have a different perspective when it comes to thinking about the ROI they get from professional development. One report (Education Policy Institute, 2021b) has posited that the systemic benefits of high quality professional development for teachers are defined by:

1 the positive impact high quality professional development has on teacher quality and therefore student attainment;
2 the positive impact it has on teacher wellbeing and therefore teacher retention.

From an individual school perspective, it is likely that ROI in CPD is viewed through the additional lenses of the extent to which it allows the school to achieve its declared improvement priorities, as well as the extent to which it contributes to favourable judgements by external inspection bodies.

Later chapters will present the case that a coaching-based approach to professional development in schools has a greater impact than other forms of CPD on all the areas referenced above, namely:

- teacher quality;
- student attainment;
- teacher wellbeing;
- teacher retention;
- school improvement;
- external inspection judgements.

But before we look in detail at the evidence for this claim, we will lay out what a coaching-based approach to professional development in schools may actually consist of. This is important, not least because of the sometimes confusing language which is often used to describe coaching in schools, as well as the differing perceptions as to what the approach actually involves.

First of all, and crucially, it is important to state that *coaching in schools should not be conflated with performance management or appraisal of employees.* The terms 'performance management' and 'appraisal' tend to be used interchangeably and usually refer to a system for assessing the overall performance of teachers and leaders. Such systems allow schools to check that expected standards are being reached, as well as to identify areas of improvement. In some education systems, the outcomes of appraisals are used to make decisions about performance-related pay. Appraisal systems may also be linked to arrangements used to manage situations where professionals are falling below the expected level of competence (capability procedures).

Appraisal processes differ between schools and education systems but the following characteristics are common to many:

- they include a relationship between an appraisee and an appraiser (in a more senior role);
- they are cyclical;
- they involve objectives which are set with/for the appraisee (often related to school priorities);
- they involve classroom observations and feedback;
- they involve collection of data which are used to make judgements about quality of teaching.

School coaching systems appear in many ways to be very much like appraisal systems. You can see from the list of characteristics of typical coaching systems below, how similar they can at first appear to be (I have highlighted differences from appraisal in bold)

- they include a relationship between a coach and a coachee (sometimes, in a more senior role);
- they are cyclical;
- they involve objectives which are set with a coachee (sometimes related to school priorities);
- they involve classroom observations and feedback;
- they involve collection of data, which are used to identify areas for development and the impact of changes in practice.

Although the similarities are plain to see, especially in terms of the structure and formats of both systems, there is one crucial distinction; whereas appraisal is primarily concerned with holding teachers to account for the quality of their work (are they good enough?), coaching is primarily focused on supporting teachers to improve their practice (how can they get better?).

A useful analogy to use, when thinking about the differences between appraisal and coaching, is the contrasting functions of summative and formative assessment of students. Summative assessments allow teachers to check what students know/can do at the end of a period of learning. These assessments are quite often high stakes, in that students can pass or fail, with positive or negative implications for their immediate and long-term futures. In the same way, appraisal systems, although they may have developmental aspects to them, are more focused on what a teacher's strengths and weaknesses are at a given time. As with summative assessments, appraisals can be seen as being high stakes, in that good or poor judgements may have positive or negative implications for professionals in terms of pay or ongoing employment. On the other hand, formative assessment is not focused on measuring student performance, rather, it is about teachers using 'in the moment' strategies to gauge what their students do or don't understand, or can or can't do, in order to make necessary adjustments to their teaching. Crucially, students should be involved in the process of formative assessment and by developing their metacognitive skills, they will be able to identify, and work to develop, their strengths and weaknesses. Like formative assessment, coaching is developmental and not focused on measuring performance. Coachees work with their coach to identify areas in which to improve their practice, and using

Table 2.1 Differences between appraisal and coaching

Appraisal	Coaching
High stakes	Low stakes
Main purpose: accountability	Main purpose: development
Observations gather data for judgement	Observations gather data for improvement
Hierarchical relationship	Partnership relationship

their coach as a resource, strive to develop in these areas in a safe, low-stakes environment.

Table 2.1 summarises the main differences between appraisal/ performance management and coaching.

It is important to make clear that appraisal/performance management has a role to play in schools, as a part of a robust approach to quality assurance. Indeed, appraisal systems are often statutory requirements for schools. The argument being made here is that schools should not conflate appraisal and coaching. These are different processes serving different functions. This means that schools need to think carefully about who is involved in delivering these systems. Ideally, the roles of appraiser and coach should be allocated to different people, but if this is not possible, clear and transparent boundaries should be established between the roles. As we have already seen, coaching is defined by the quality of the relationship between the coach and coachee. This relationship should be characterised by trust, openness and authenticity. It is difficult to capture these qualities if the outcomes of the process have high-stakes consequences for one of the parties; indeed, doubt, caution, and even fear are more likely to be present than trust, openness and authenticity, if the process has implications for tenure or income.

So, having established that coaching in schools is not appraisal in disguise, and should be focused on helping education professionals get better at their job, rather than making judgements about their performance, we will now spend some time understanding the different ways in which a coaching approach can manifest itself in these settings.

The model in Figure 2.1 suggests four possible dimensions of coaching in schools, which may be deployed according to the role and level of expertise/experience of the coachee.

The next section of this chapter explores each of these dimensions of coaching in turn. We will look at the main features of each

Figure 2.1 Dimensions of coaching in schools

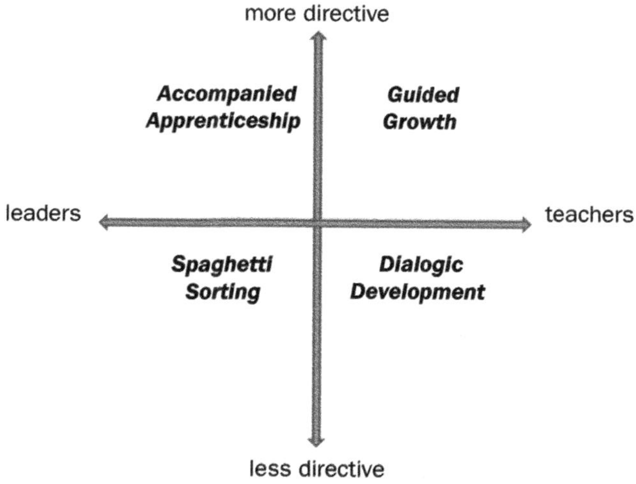

approach, consider when and how they may be best deployed, and link them to studies and coaching models which are used by schools to guide practice.

We begin with coaching approaches which are focused on school leaders' development.

Coaching for school leaders

It has long been known that those in leadership positions in schools are subject to a whole range of pressures and strains. Among the things that have been identified as making school leadership particularly challenging are the loneliness and emotional turmoil that come with such roles, as well as the overwhelming complexity of the institutions they work in. It has been reported (Lofthouse and Whiteside, 2020) that coaching for school leaders can alleviate such challenges by, among other things, providing emotional support, improving working relationships, developing problem-solving skills, and increasing confidence. Certainly, in my own experience as a coach to school leaders, those I have worked with have found the process to be very useful, not least in that it provides a 'protected space' where they are able to think deeply about issues facing them and make plans to move forward positively.

There is currently little data providing insight into the numbers of headteachers and school senior leaders receiving coaching, but given the positive experiences that many report, and the wider impact coaching appears to have on schools as a result of leaders' improved decision-making and communication (Raybould et al., 2021), there is a strong argument for making leadership coaching a norm in schools.

There is, however, a question to be asked about who should be doing this coaching of school leaders. Certainly, within the corporate executive coaching sphere, the question of whether it is better for leaders to have access to internal coaches (i.e. company employees), or external coaches (i.e. contracted providers) is a commonly asked one. When internal provision is preferred, it is usually because of the low direct costs involved and the fact that the coaches will know the company context; while companies opting for external provision usually do so because they value the independent input and the neutral space provided for coachees. Within the school sector, however, there seems to be a consensus that 'external is best' but only if providers have experience of school leadership themselves, as well as coaching credentials. Reasons cited for this preference include: the resulting provision of a 'safe' confidential space, and the fact that such coaches understand the complexities of school leadership but have no vested interest in the issues being explored (Lofthouse and Whiteside, 2020).

So, having established the value of coaching for school leaders, let us now look at two possible ways of delivering this.

Leadership coaching: Accompanied Apprenticeship

The Accompanied Apprenticeship approach is most appropriately deployed when working with 'novices', school leaders who are new to the role or education professionals who are aspiring to leadership positions. The role of coach here is usually taken by a more experienced peer, often in an equivalent or similar role in another school.

The Accompanied Apprenticeship approach recognises that as an inexperienced or aspiring leader, the coachee has much to learn and that an ideal way for them to do this is through a relationship with a professional who 'knows the ropes'. 'Sharing' and 'advising' are the default mechanisms of Accompanied Apprenticeship. This does not suggest that the coach should adopt a micromanaging approach (What's the problem?; Here's what you should do), as this is both disempowering for the coachee and does not provide space for the reflection and connection-making needed for meaningful learning to occur.

On the other hand, a coaching approach which is purely facilitative, and which focuses on 'coaxing' the coachee to come up with strategies and solutions for development, has limited utility here. This is simply because the inexperienced coachee will not yet have developed a sophisticated enough mental model or 'schema' of school leadership for them to be able to draw on this when trying to identify appropriate goals and strategies. Psychologists describe schemas as cognitive frameworks consisting of connected knowledge. Schemas are developed through multiple experiences of making connections between pieces of knowledge. We use our existing schemas to make sense of new knowledge that is presented to us, and as we connect new knowledge and understanding to what we already have, our schemas grow. A useful metaphor for this, is the brain as a gigantic card indexing system. Schemas are the sections in this system and the cards are units of knowledge. An index card on its own will have limited meaning to us, but if we can locate the appropriate section in which to file it, and then rifle through other cards in this section, in order to make connections between those cards and the new one, the information on the index card will become more meaningful and useful. An inexperienced coachee is unlikely to have a large number of cards in the section of their mental indexing system labelled 'leadership'. Thus, the coach's role in this type of relationship is probably best focused on helping the coachee add index cards to their 'leadership section', by sharing their knowledge and experience and helping the coachee reflect on this in the light of their particular needs and priorities. To adopt a purely facilitative approach in this type of relationship is less likely to bear fruit, because the coachee has insufficient prior knowledge to effectively identify appropriate strategies and courses of action open to them, and this is likely to lead to frustration for both parties.

It has been suggested that effective support provided by experienced school leaders to novice school leaders will consist of: guidance (through words and actions), facilitation (of enriching relationships), and input (of effective leadership practices) (O'Mahony, 2004). Another useful model which has been used to frame this type of coaching relationship (Anderson and Shannon, 1988) identifies the following functions of the coach: to teach (by modelling, informing, addressing misconceptions, diagnosing and questioning); to sponsor (by advocating and supporting); to encourage (by recognising achievements, inspiring and challenging); to counsel (by listening, probing, reflecting, clarifying and advising); and to befriend (by accepting and empathising).

My own view is that, given their particular needs, a novice leader will benefit particularly from an approach that focuses specifically on building competence *and* confidence. As well as lacking knowledge and experience in the field, the responsibility and complexity involved in such roles can lead novice leaders to feel vulnerable and unprepared. Therefore, it is the coach's job to both contribute to the coachee's developing knowledge base and to build their self-esteem by celebrating achievements and by putting setbacks in perspective, while also using these as learning opportunities.

In addition, a coach working with a novice leader will need to ensure they are not contributing to a coachee's sense of being overwhelmed. This becomes a risk if too much ground is covered too quickly, as the coach shares their knowledge, experience and ideas with the coachee. Following their coachee's agenda, a skilled coach will focus in on a particular area of practice and support the coachee to become more confident and competent in that area, before then moving on.

To use another metaphor, if we regard school leadership as being akin to the façade of a cathedral, fascinating and beautiful even, but also multi-faceted and complex, we can see the coach as a master builder, supporting their apprentice (coachee) to construct their own façade. The master builder and apprentice work together on a particular section of the façade, the master builder sharing relevant skills and knowledge, encouraging the apprentice when something goes wrong and praising them for a particularly well-rendered piece of work. Once this section is complete, apprentice and master move on to the next and then the next. All the time, the master builder is aware that this façade belongs to the apprentice. By fostering competence and confidence in their apprentice, the aim is to create a sense of pride and achievement in the work they have done, so that in the future they are able to operate independently, even going on to become master builders themselves, ready to share their expertise with their own generation of apprentices.

Leadership coaching: Spaghetti Sorting

Warren Buffett, the famous business magnate, investor and philanthropist, has been quoted as saying, 'It always amazes me how many seemingly intelligent people have trouble thinking clearly. Their thoughts get tangled into a plate of spaghetti' (Einhorn, 2018).

Due to the extremely challenging nature of the role, school leaders' plates of spaghetti are often particularly tangled. The range and quantity of areas covered by the UK government's Headteacher

Standards (Department for Education, 2020) give some insight into the reasons for this. Among the many areas listed that headteachers ultimately have responsibility for are:

- creating and maintaining a culture of high expectations;
- ensuring all teaching is of high quality;
- providing a rich, broad and balanced curriculum;
- establishing effective behaviour management systems;
- ensuring all children with special educational needs and disabilities are properly provided for;
- ensuring the provision of good quality professional development for all staff;
- ensuring the protection and safety of all members of the school community;
- managing finances effectively;
- ensuring the smooth running of day-to-day procedures;
- ensuring the school is focused on continuous improvement;
- forging and maintaining partnerships;
- being accountable to governors and other bodies, including inspecting organisations.

This already wide-ranging list of responsibilities does not even take into account the 'mission creep' that the role of a school leader is often subject to. A good example of this took place during the COVID-19 pandemic, when many headteachers around the world found themselves responsible for overseeing remote learning arrangements, establishing 'bio-bubbles' and social distancing measures, and even administering virus testing.

Reading all of this, it is easy to understand why 89 per cent of senior leaders in schools have reported experiencing significant levels of stress, which have had a negative impact on their sleep, concentration and mood (Education Support, 2021). We will focus in greater detail on the links between coaching and wellbeing in Chapter 4 but we will now consider the role the approach can play in helping to untangle the mountain of spaghetti school leaders are often presented with.

The model I most commonly draw on, when coaching experienced headteachers, is the BASIC Method (Buck, 2020). BASIC was developed by a well-respected educator, who has, over the years, gained significant insight into what coaching approaches work best when working with school leaders.

Like GROW and other coaching models, BASIC is a mnemonic which provides a structure for coaching conversations, in this case standing for: **B**ackground, **A**im, **S**trategy, **I**mplementation and **C**ommitment. What I find particularly useful about BASIC, is its placing of the 'Background' stage at the very beginning of the coaching process. By contrast, other models often propose that an exploration of the coachee's current context or reality takes place *after* a goal has been established. Buck's model places importance on an open-ended exploration of the coachee's current situation before a goal is set. This provides an opportunity to begin to untangle some of the coachee's spaghetti prior to an agenda being set for the rest of the process.

When coaching, I will tend to spend at least one or two sessions with a coachee, exploring their current professional situation. The result of this can be that the coachee ends up identifying a goal which is different from that they may originally have had in mind. This often comes about because of a 'not seeing the wood for the trees' scenario. School leaders can be so caught up in day-to-day fire-fighting and general busy-ness that they simply do not have the time to think things through. In other words, to refer again to Daniel Kahneman's work, they are tending to spend a lot of time using the fast, intuitive System 1 thinking that responds to the most immediately discernible characteristics of a situation. Through the careful deployment of questions, a skilled coach can create a space where a coachee uses System 2 thinking to go beyond the surface features of a scenario and analyses more deeply what is really going on.

Questions that encourage this type of System 2 thinking during the Background stage of BASIC, may include:

- What's on your mind at the moment?
- What other elements are relevant to this situation?
- What are the push and pull factors?
- What have you tried so far?
- How has your thinking about this evolved?
- What differing perspectives may others have?
- What other factors may be in play here?
- Anything else?
- Anything else?

The Aim, Implementation and Commitment stages of BASIC have strong parallels with the Goal, Options and Will elements of the GROW model, in that they focus in on setting a goal, exploring possible actions, agreeing which of these best serve the goal, creating a plan, and then building commitment to follow through on this. However, I would like now to focus on the Strategy phase of BASIC, as, again, I think it has particular importance for school leaders, coping with demanding and highly complex roles.

In his book, *Good Strategy, Bad Strategy*, Richard Rumelt (2012) identifies three core elements of effective strategy: diagnosis, guiding policy and coherent action.

Diagnosis for Rumelt is the simplification of a complex situation through the identification of its most critical elements. The exploratory Background stage of the coaching process will have laid the ground for diagnosis and the establishment of an Aim will have provided a context. At this stage, the coach may say something like: 'We know something about your big picture, you've decided what you want to achieve, now let's identify which are the most critical elements you need to consider in order to move forward.'

Having established what these critical elements are (and these may be enabling factors, as well as obstacles), the coach and coachee move on to creating a guiding policy or template for overcoming the obstacles or enhancing the enablers. This is really an overarching approach or direction of travel and should be defined in language which is focused and concise.

Lastly, the guiding policy is used to frame a coherent plan of action, ideally with time frames, roles and responsibilities and resources all clearly defined.

To illustrate what this process might look like, let's imagine a coachee has decided to work with the EXACT Goal we used as an example in Chapter 1: 'everyone knows, everyone understands' (this was related to improving communication between senior leaders and staff). With the coach's prompting, the coachee identifies the following 'critical elements' in relation to this goal: teachers have expressed frustration at not understanding why certain initiatives have been introduced; the previous headteacher was seen to have a very open-door to all staff; the current head has tried to replicate this but found it unsustainable; there are many meetings per week in the school; these meetings often overrun; they can also get heated; some Heads of Year seem to communicate effectively with their teams; not all teachers seem to read or respond to emails. Having discussed these, the coachee identifies the following strategy: learn from what has worked and is working to develop new school-wide protocols and expectations. This overarching approach is then used to create a coherent plan of action, which includes a whole staff survey, the establishment of a working party to make recommendations on new protocols and expectations regarding meetings and emails (and which includes those Heads of Year who are seen to communicate effectively with their teams); the introduction of time-limited agenda items in meetings; and a termly Q and A with senior leaders and the whole staff. You will no doubt note that the creation of a plan of action coincides with the Implementation stage of the BASIC method, which focuses on what the coachee will do to deliver their strategy.

This example shows how coaching can help a more experienced leader make sense of the spaghetti on their plate. The job of the coach is to provide the coachee with the headspace and prompting to do the 'hard thinking' that enables them to identify priorities, understand better the nature of the challenges they face, and to think positively about how they can move forward. If the coaching is provided by someone with knowledge of, and experience in school leadership themselves, there may also be moments when the sharing of ideas and suggestions would be appropriate and useful to the coachee, but the coach should avoid 'imposing' these and the default approach should be to provide a sounding board first and foremost.

Coaching for teachers

The coaching approaches outlined above are certainly applicable when it comes to teachers in schools. Teachers can and do benefit from the wide-ranging conversations that models such as GROW and BASIC can provide. However, the type of coaching that teachers are most likely to experience, and the one which we focus on in the following sections, is often referred to as 'instructional coaching'. Of all the terminology surrounding coaching in schools, 'instructional coaching' is probably the phrase that most often leads to confusion and differing interpretations. This has much to do with the word 'instructional', which can be understood as referring to the role of the coach (I instruct, you do), or as relating to instruction as a synonym for teaching (coaching that relates to classroom practice). My own interpretation of the term is more in line with the second; although, as will become apparent, there are models of instructional coaching that do indeed frame a directive approach, where the coach could be seen to be 'instructing' their coachee what to do. In order to avoid some of this confusion, for the purposes of this book, we will not use the term 'instructional coaching' and instead refer to 'coaching for teachers'. The definition we will use for this is below.

Coaching for teachers: A professional relationship often, but not always, involving a more and less experienced practitioner, where cycles of observation, feedback, reflection and goal-setting are used to incrementally improve teaching and student outcomes.

The roots of teacher coaching as professional development are found in the work of Dr Jim Knight in the late part of the twentieth century. In 1999, Knight presented a paper called 'Partnership learning: Putting conversation at the heart of professional development'. In this he outlined the principles and structures underpinning an approach to professional development based on dialogue, which was trialled in a number of settings and its impact compared with that of more traditional teacher training models. The results of this suggested that partnership learning was comparatively more engaging, more likely to lead to teachers implementing target practices and the experience more likely to be remembered (Knight, 1999).

Since then, coaching for teachers has spread widely as a practice in schools around the world. An OECD report (2018) found that two-thirds of schools in member countries had some sort of coaching or mentoring programme, and that these were becoming increasingly commonplace.

As coaching for teachers has grown as a professional development practice, so have the number of approaches and models that guide this practice proliferated. Roughly speaking, these various models can be divided into two types:

1 A largely directive style of coaching, which draws heavily on the sharing of expertise, referred to here as *Guided Growth*.
2 A more facilitative style of coaching, which is in line with Jim Knight's early (and indeed later) work, referred to here as *Dialogic Development*.

These models tend to follow similar cyclical processes, typically based on the following type of structure:

> observation or sharing of practice – feedback/reflection – planning for improvement – implementation of planned improvement – observation or sharing of practice

However, despite these structural commonalities, there are marked practical and philosophical differences between the Guided Growth and Dialogic Development styles of coaching for teachers. In order to understand these, as well as to gain insight into their possible utility in different contexts, the last part of this chapter will compare and contrast two specific models illustrating the Guided Growth and Dialogic Development categories: Incremental Coaching (Ambition Institute, 2017), and the Impact Cycle (Knight, 2018).

Coaching for teachers: Guided Growth (incremental coaching)

Description of the approach

This model of teacher coaching, developed by the Ambition Institute based on the work of Paul Bambrick-Santoyo (2018) and the Uncommon Schools group of charter schools in the US, is now implemented in a number of schools and academy trusts in the UK. The process is tightly structured and focused on one specific area of teaching practice at a time. Coaches tend to be trained senior or middle leaders (but often not line managers to the coachees), with a track record of good classroom practice.

The process involves the coach observing the coachee teach a lesson, initially focusing their attention on a particular (previously agreed) area of practice. A strictly timed feedback meeting led by the coach and framed by the 'See it, Name it, Do It' approach (Bambrick-Santoyo, 2018), is held soon after. This is structured in the following way:

1 *See it*

    1a. *Identify past success.* Focused on the previously agreed area of focus/action step.

    Example: 'We spoke last time about the importance of 'cold calling' when seeking answers to your questions, and how this prevents students opting out of thinking about what you've asked. I noticed that you used this throughout the discussion and brought in nearly all the students. How did that feel? Do you think you're ready to move on to a new action step?'

    1b. *See the new area of focus and the gap.* This introduces a new development area the coach has identified as a result of observing the teacher.

    Example: 'Today I'd like us to look at how effective modelling by the teacher helps students understand new processes and skills. What do you think are the keys to this? Why is this important? What do you think is the gap between the way you introduced (new skill) yesterday and the best practice model?'

2 *Name it*

    2a. *Name the action step.* This provides the new area of focus for the coachee.

Example: 'Based on our discussion, what do you think your next action step should be? What will you need to do differently? So, let's confirm the action step.'

3 *Do it*

> 3a. *Plan and practise.* This allows the coachee to decide when they will implement the action step and to practise doing so.

Example: 'When will you be able to do this in your upcoming lessons? Let's go over the action step again. Now let's practise, show me how you'll do this.'

> 3b. *Agree follow-up.* This wraps up the session and commits coach and coachee to follow-up.

Example: 'When would be the best time for me to come and observe this? Would it be helpful to observe me/another teacher using this technique?'

Each stage of the meeting is given a time limit and it is intended that the whole process lasts no longer than 40 minutes.

Important features of this approach to emphasise include:

- a sharp focus on one development area/action step at a time (new steps are only agreed when the coachee has embedded the previous area of focus into their practice);
- the importance of compliance with agreements and time frames;
- the importance of short time intervals between different stages.

Possible advantages of the Guided Growth approach

1 Effective use of time is an important feature of this model and its efficient and streamlined structure means that schools can usually build it into timetables with limited disruption.
2 The focus on one development area at a time avoids the 'scatter-gun' checklist approach where observed teachers get feedback on multiple areas of practice, and which risks them becoming cognitively overloaded (see Chapter 6) and ultimately overwhelmed.
3 Inexperienced or less confident teachers may especially benefit from the highly structured nature of Guided Growth approaches, in the same way that students who are being introduced to, or struggling to learn, new skills often benefit from scaffolding provided by the teacher.

Possible disadvantages of the Guided Growth approach

1 The highly structured nature of the approach and semi-scripted feedback may be off-putting to some teachers, especially those with more experience.

2 The approach could be seen as simplistic, not accounting for the highly complex nature of teaching and our ever-evolving understanding of what works in the classroom.

3 Practising teaching in front of a colleague may be difficult for some teachers, especially those from less demonstrative cultures.

4 The approach limits the scope for reflection on the part of the coachee.

When might this be a useful approach to deploy?

A Guided Growth approach to coaching may be particularly suited for use with teachers who are new to the profession. As we explored earlier in relation to novice school leaders, teachers who are in the early stages of their career will not yet have developed mental models that guide their classroom practice. The structured approach provided by Guided Growth coaching models provides an opportunity for inexperienced teachers to learn, implement and receive feedback on new techniques in a focused and incremental manner. It is no coincidence that the Early Career Framework, a two-year induction scheme for new teachers launched in England in 2021, has at its heart a mentoring programme which in its design, draws heavily on Guided Growth-type approaches.

However, it can be argued that Guided Growth approaches to coaching are too prescriptive or 'top-down', and do not place enough emphasis on a coachee's own perspectives about their practice. This viewpoint would suggest that a teacher's independent professionalism is undermined by an approach that essentially tells them what they must change and what they must do to correct this.

My own view is that Guided Growth models do have a place within a coaching approach to professional development in a school, but that they should be deployed only as and when appropriate, as defined by teachers' preferences, needs and stages of professional growth. If used as a default model for all teachers in a school, there is a risk that some will feel micromanaged and even patronised by the process. The disaffection that is likely to be a result of this would clearly be counterproductive in a process designed to facilitate professional development.

Coaching for teachers: Dialogic Development (the Impact Cycle)

Description of the approach

A Dialogic Development style of coaching for teachers places greater emphasis on the insights and reflections of the coachee than a Guided Growth approach. This is not to say the coach has no role to play in identifying areas for improvement or suggesting ideas, but this type of process is more based on shared thinking than it is on handed-down practice.

Jim Knight's Impact Cycle (2018) grew out of his extensive experience of coaching teachers and years of researching the practice. The approach is based on the concept of partnership and seven principles which Knight developed in his pioneering teacher coaching work nearly 20 years earlier: equality, choice, voice, dialogue, reflection, praxis and reciprocity.

The Impact Cycle is made up of three stages and nine sub-stages. These are summarised below.

1 *Identify*

    1a. *Current reality.* Coach and coachee reflect together on a video of a lesson (if this is possible) and through dialogue, an area for improvement is identified.

    Example: 'Which one aspect of this lesson would you want to improve in order for it to have a greater impact on student learning?'

    1b. *Goal.* A goal, which is focused and measurable by impact on students, is identified.

    Example: 'OK, we've decided on improving the impact of your modelling of new skills and processes to students: how will you know you have been successful in this? How can we quantify the impact on the students?'

    1c. *Teaching strategy.* At this stage, the coach is likely to suggest some strategies that may help the coachee reach their goal. These are not imposed but are offered on the basis that the coach is likely to have a wider range of experience and knowledge to draw on.

    Example: 'I have some suggestions that may be helpful here. One strategy you may find useful is backward fading. Have you got any ideas about this?'

2 *Learn*

2d. *Modelling.* This in effect fulfils the function of a worked example for a teacher. The coach offers to model a technique for the coachee to observe. This may happen via video, in either the coach's or the coachee's class or via co-teaching.

Example: 'Let's arrange a time when I can come into your class and demonstrate this.'

2e. *Checklists.* Knight refers to the usefulness of a 'playbook', a manual made up of good practice checklists, which can be used as a common reference point by all coaches and coachees in a school. Many schools I have worked with find the Teaching Walkthrus series to be useful for this purpose (Sherrington and Caviglioli, 2020).

Example: 'The 5 steps in the "live modelling" Teaching Walkthru may be useful here, let's have a look together.'

3 *Improve*

3f. *Direction.* This stage takes place after the coachee has tried out the previously discussed strategies and ideas in their classroom and refers to checking on the direction of the coaching conversations. Knight points out here that if the coachee wishes to discuss something outside of the Impact Cycle, they should be invited to do so, thereby emphasising that the coach does not 'own' the process.

Example: 'What would you like to talk about today? How are you finding these sessions?'

3g. *Progress.* At this stage, the coach and coachee will discuss whether the goal has been achieved, referring to any data that has been gathered. If the goal has been reached, the coach will ask the coachee if they wish to set a new goal and may then begin the cycle again.

Example: 'What's gone well? Have you encountered any problems? How can you tell you've reached/not reached your goal? What progress are you noting?'

3h. *Improvements.* Building on the previous stage, coach and coachee decide whether 'tweaks' or 'major overhauls' may be needed in the process.

Example: 'How might you adapt the strategy? What other approach could you take? To what extent is the way we framed this goal serving your purpose? What changes are you going to make?'

3i. *Actions.* This final stage is very similar to the Will stage of GROW and the Commitment stage of BASIC. At this point coach and coachee summarise and confirm what will happen next, while committing to the actions that have been agreed.

Example: 'Let's go over what we've spoken about and agreed. Can you foresee any difficulties? What excites you about these next steps?'

Possible advantages of the Dialogic Development approach

1 Engagement and commitment on the part of the coachee are likely to be high if Partnership Principles are being followed.
2 As with Guided Growth models, the emphasis on focused areas of practice and specific feedback reduces the potential for cognitive overload.
3 A coachee involved in a dialogic coaching relationship will be required to think hard, and this in itself can lead to meaningful professional learning being facilitated because of the principle of 'desirable difficulty' (see Chapter 5).

Possible disadvantages of the Dialogic Development approach

1 The approach may be time-consuming.
2 Less experienced teachers may not have sufficient prior knowledge to engage meaningfully in dialogic inquiry about their practice.
3 The heavy emphasis on videoing lessons may create issues related to data protection, logistics or teacher discomfort with recording their practice.

When might this be a useful approach to deploy?

Experienced teachers or indeed inexperienced teachers who have quickly developed a good level of knowledge and confidence may benefit from this style of coaching. This approach is in line with that of academic inquiry, as traditionally practised in university courses, and many professionals will thrive under such conditions. But it should also be remembered that even experienced teachers may sometimes prefer and benefit from the more directive option offered by Guided Growth coaching models.

3 The case for coaching as professional development

Having explored differing dimensions of coaching in school settings, we now focus on the case for placing coaching at the centre of professional development programmes for teachers and school leaders. We will do this by analysing a range of research studies and reviews through the lenses of these questions:

- To what extent is a coaching approach to professional development for educators in line with what we know about best practice in CPD?
- What impact does coaching for teachers and school leaders have on practice and student learning?

A key report for us to focus on here was produced by the Teacher Development Trust (Cordingley et al., 2015), and reviewed international evidence on the characteristics of effective CPD in schools. Here we take each of the main findings from this report and give them a RAG (red, amber, green) rating, based on the extent to which coaching (in any of the four dimensions already explored) can be said to be in line with the report's findings.

1 CPD interventions that produce profound and enduring change in practice tend to have a duration of more than a year and no less than two terms, as well as a 'rhythm' of follow-up and consolidation. *GREEN*: All of the coaching approaches to professional development already explored are cyclical in nature and will ideally be built into systems and routines so that teachers and/or leaders have access to regular and ongoing opportunities to reflect on their practice and take action to improve it.

2 Content is relevant to participants' needs and priorities. *GREEN*: This is one of the fundamental characteristics of coaching; as we

have seen, identification of individual needs and priorities is a central part of any coaching process.

3　CPD interventions which are aligned and create a shared sense of purpose in a school are more impactful. *AMBER*: At first glance, due to its focus on the individual, this characteristic seems to have nothing at all in common with a coaching approach to PD. However, if we consider a whole school commitment to coaching to be in itself an example of a shared sense of purpose, it could be argued that the approach is at least partially in line with this characteristic. A school-wide understanding of and willingness to engage in continuous incremental improvement through coaching, may have the same galvanising effect as commitment to any other practice.

4　Programmes focus on both subject knowledge and pedagogy. *GREEN*: Coaching programmes for teachers, whether they are of the more or less directive type, should embrace practitioners' knowledge of their subject as well as their classroom practice.

5　Successful PD programmes involve teachers using input to experiment in their classrooms, engaging with research evidence and assessment data in order to gauge the impact of these experiments. *GREEN*: Robust coaching cycles will involve teachers trying out new practices, drawing on research in the identification of these and student data to understand their impact.

6　External and internal providers of CPD have relevant specialist knowledge and build trusting relationships with participants, where challenge and support are central to the process. *GREEN*: As explored earlier, trust, challenge and support are central to any productive coaching relationship, so we can say the approach appears to be, at least partially, in line with this characteristic. I would also suggest that because of the highly specialised nature of teaching and school leadership, expertise is also an important feature of effective coaching in school settings. This is definitely the case when it comes to coaching which is related to classroom practice; and although some proponents of executive coaching in a wider sense insist that expertise is not essential in a coach, as they are only fulfilling a facilitative role, I have already argued that knowledge and experience are in fact important for a school leader coach to have so that appropriate guidance can be offered as and when it is needed.

7　Professional collaboration focused on problem solving and improving student learning is built into the process of PD. *GREEN*: Clearly, this is central to the DNA of coaching in schools.

Mechanisms

Another summary of factors contributing to effective professional development, published more recently by the Educational Endowment Foundation (2021), identified four 'mechanisms' or building blocks that effective PD programmes include. These are listed below:

1 *Build knowledge* by managing cognitive load, revisiting prior learning.
2 *Motivate staff* by setting/agreeing on goals, presenting information from credible sources, providing affirmation and reinforcement after progress.
3 *Develop teaching techniques* through instruction, social support, modelling, monitoring/feedback, rehearsal.
4 *Embed practice* by providing prompts/cues, prompting action planning, encouraging monitoring, prompting context-specific repetition.

Hopefully the reader will note immediately that these mechanisms and their component parts are all central features of teacher coaching programmes.

This EEF report was partially informed by a study (Sims and Fletcher-Wood, 2021), which cast doubt on the robustness and inference processes of previous reviews of effective professional development. The authors believed that this had resulted in the development of a consensus on what constitutes best practice PD, without sufficient evidence for this actually being present. In order for future reviews to be more robust, they called for those focused on direct evidence of impact on student learning to be combined with what behavioural and cognitive science tell us about how professionals learn and as a result change their practice. The mechanisms outlined in the EEF report are in line with the second part of this recommendation but the call for inclusion of clear evidence of impact on student learning is not responded to in the EEF report.

As it happens, being able to establish a direct and clear connection between teacher development programmes and a resultant impact on student learning is very difficult to do with any great certitude. The fact that the teacher provides a degree of separation between the original intervention (PD programme) and what is being measured to ascertain impact (student learning), makes it challenging to prove causal links. Moreover, the 'noisiness' of teaching, i.e. the sheer number of factors in play in a classroom that have an impact on how well students are learning (from pedagogical approaches to a wasp flying into the room), provides a further barrier to understanding whether a professional development intervention is having an impact on student outcomes.

We look now at findings from three types of research which may mitigate some of the difficulties around ascertaining the impact of teacher learning on student learning. One is meta-analysis, where the results of multiple studies are combined in order to derive a pooled estimate of the level of effect of a type of intervention. The second is randomised control trials, an experimental form of research, which has its roots in medical science. And the third is A/B testing where two types of intervention are trialled with two similar groups and the results compared.

John Hattie's work in the field of meta-analyses relating to the impact of different factors on student achievement, is as well known as it is extensive. Hattie is constantly updating his work, adding more and more studies and influencing factors to his huge database. At time of writing, Hattie ranks 252 factors by impact on student outcomes. At the top of this list, generating by far the greatest impact is 'collective teacher efficacy' (Hattie, 2019). A slippery beast to define, collective teacher efficacy is described by Hattie as teachers in a school having high expectations for student learning, and a belief that, fed by use of data to monitor the impact of practice, they can work as a group to deliver those high expectations (Hattie, 2018). With its focus on collaboration, reflection and data-informed decision-making, coaching for teachers can be understood as a vehicle for collective teacher efficacy (CTE). Indeed, it has been suggested that there are four sources of collective efficacy (Hoogsteen, 2020), all of which can be generated through good coaching practice:

1 Mastery experiences: a collective sense of success.
2 Vicarious experiences: skill being effectively modelled by someone else.
3 Social persuasion: feedback from colleagues.
4 Affective states: optimism in the face of complex or stressful situations.

The links between collective teacher efficacy and teacher coaching are clear to see. Given the number 1 ranking Hattie gives CTE in terms of its impact on student learning, it is tempting to say that we now have all we need to make the case for coaching in schools. However, a word of caution: in recent times some have begun to question Hattie's methodology, both in terms of how effect sizes are ascertained and how they are reported (Lilley, 2016). Indeed, Hattie himself has now moved away from the ranking of effect sizes, recognising that this was leading to practitioners making superficial judgements, which prevent them from delving into the 'stories' behind the data (Lovell, n.d.). This does not mean we should dismiss Hattie's meta-analyses out of hand, rather, that we should avoid regarding them as providing definitive proof of impact. Taken in this way, his work provides us with a degree of useful insight into why a coaching approach may positively impact student learning.

Another significant meta-analysis to note, before we move on to randomised control trial studies, was carried out in the USA and focused specifically on studies on the effect of teacher coaching programmes on student achievement (Kraft et al., 2018). Drawing together the results of 31 studies, the researchers concluded that coaching for teachers generally improved student learning, with this being especially the case for small-scale programmes and those focused on the teaching of specific subjects.

Randomised control trials (RCTs) are often referred to as the 'gold standard' in educational research. Widely used in clinical trials to measure the effects of drugs and medical procedures, an RCT seeks to ascertain the impact of an intervention by applying it in an 'experimental group' and comparing the results generated with those from a 'control group', which has not received the intervention. RCTs are sometimes criticised when used in educational settings. This can be for ethical reasons (as not all children receive a potentially beneficial intervention); for reasons of validity (as the complex nature of classrooms makes it difficult to claim that any observed differences between the groups are definitely due to the intervention); for reasons of developer interest (if the organisation running the trials has a stake in the intervention); or because of poor implementation (due to badly conceived delivery models, size of groups or problems with timing). However, even when taking into account all of these caveats, I tend to agree with Kevan Collins, CEO of the Education Endowment Foundation, when he says, 'Randomised trials are rarely perfect, but they are currently the best way we know of generating reliable evidence that teachers can consistently use to enable us to improve the education of … children' (2017, p. 13).

Probably the most significant RCT on the effect of teacher coaching on student attainment was carried out to assess the impact of a video-based coaching programme focused on developing the quality of teachers' interactions with secondary school students (Allen et al., 2011). Some 78 teachers of different subjects were randomly assigned to a control group, which received a standard year-long professional development programme, or an experiment group, which received training and follow-up coaching based on reflection on the nature and quality of the teacher's relationship with their students. Students in both groups were tested before the programme, at the end of the programme, and again during the following academic year. Results showed insignificant comparative gains in student attainment at the end of the programme but substantial gains when the students were tested again the following year. What makes this experiment particularly interesting is that four years later, it was replicated (with one change being that the programme was extended to two years, with less regular touchpoints between coach and coachee) and generated similar gains in student attainment.

The fact that this study was replicated, generating similar outcomes means that we can regard the results as being reliable. However, a question remains about whether this experiment actually tells us more about the impact of good relationships with students, than it does about the impact of coaching for teachers as a form of professional development. The authors do not say anything about the content or form of the control group's professional development, but the assumption is that it did not have a focus on improving student-teacher interactions. Given this, it is difficult to tell whether: (1) the improvement in student grades was because the teachers got better at establishing positive relationships with their students, or whether (2) the improvement in student grades was because teachers got better at establishing positive relationships with their students, which was in turn because of the coaching they received.

The results of a study carried out in Argentina (Albornoz et al., 2017) may provide us with more insight into the effects on student learning of a coaching approach to professional development, as opposed to a traditional training approach. This piece of research used A/B testing to assess the impact of different approaches to PD on student learning in science.

Some 70 schools were randomly assigned to one of three groups, and the Grade 7 science teachers in each of these received either:

1 A four-hour training session on teaching the human body.
2 A four-hour training session on teaching the human body, plus a structured curriculum in this area.
3 A four-hour training session on teaching the human body, plus a structured curriculum in this area, plus 12 hour-long sessions with a teacher coach.

All students were then tested on their scientific knowledge and skills. The results showed that students of teachers in groups (2) and (3) performed significantly better than those in group (1), but that there was little difference between the test scores of the students taught in groups (1) and (2). The exception to this was with relatively inexperienced teachers, where coaching was seen to have a significant impact on student test scores.

The researchers concluded that a training programme complemented with a structured curriculum is a cost-effective way of raising student attainment but that an additional coaching programme is only worthwhile if it is implemented with inexperienced teachers. It should be said here that an important detail, not contained in the research paper, is a description of the nature of the coaching that was carried out. I would speculate that the coaching approach used is likely to have had more in common with a Guided Growth model than a Dialogic Development model, and that this may account for the greater impact seen with inexperienced teachers. Certainly, if this were to be the case, it would emphasise once again the importance of using differentiated coaching approaches, based on the needs and preferences of the coachee. Indeed, I would hypothesise that a similar study using a Dialogic Development model would have a proportionately greater impact on experienced teachers, thereby leading to better test results for their students.

Research on coaching for teachers is extensive, indeed it has been called the best evidenced category of CPD (Sims, 2018). The same cannot be said, however, for coaching for school leaders which is currently under-researched. One exception is provided by an evaluation of a year-long headteacher coaching programme carried out in the UK (Lofthouse and Whiteside, 2020). The report found that headteachers involved in the programme benefitted from systematic coaching in the following ways:

- provision of time and space for supported reflection, which would otherwise not be available;
- the opportunity to address challenges which had an impact on their wellbeing;
- development of self-belief and confidence;
- development of leadership and management capacity.

The report concluded that coaching 'proved to be a mechanism for making a difference in both the personal and professional lives of headteachers' (ibid., p. 29).

Interestingly this study also highlighted some wider implications of coaching for school leaders, suggesting that it has the potential to reduce the number of headteachers leaving the profession and that, through headteachers' improved practice, it can also have a positive impact on others in the school community.

Summary

At the beginning of this chapter, we posed the following questions:

1 To what extent is a coaching approach to professional development for educators in line with what we know about best practice in CPD?
2 What impact does coaching for teachers and school leaders have on practice and student learning?

We have seen that the characteristics and features of a coaching approach to professional development largely coincide with current thinking about what makes for effective CPD for teachers. Similarly, evidence from various research studies points to coaching for teachers and school leaders improving practice and leading to better outcomes for students.

We have also seen that these positive outcomes are very dependent on how schools make decisions as to when and in what manner coaching is deployed. The importance of this flexible and intentional deployment of coaching in schools is highlighted in another report, which concluded that the most effective coaching models tend to be bespoke, allowing for the individual and evolving contexts of schools to be considered through an iterative and collaborative approach to programme design (Hollweck and Lofthouse, 2021).

In closing this chapter, it is important to stress that the case being made here is not that coaching should completely replace professional development based on training, courses, conferences and other more 'traditional' approaches. Indeed, any form of CPD that is designed to be in line with the type of best practice guidance outlined at the beginning of this chapter is likely to have a positive impact on both teacher and student learning. Rather, I am suggesting that schools should consider how they may balance and link these two forms of professional development. If we regard traditional forms of CPD as the 'front-loading' of subject and pedagogical knowledge, and coaching as an opportunity for individuals to reflect on and make plans to put this knowledge into practice, schools are in a good position to glean maximum benefit from both approaches.

4 Coaching and wellbeing

In his book, The Outliers, Malcolm Gladwell says "It's not how much money we make that ultimately makes us happy between 9 and 5. It's whether or not our work fulfils us. Being a teacher is meaningful" (2008, p. 150). There is a great deal in this quote that resonates. Certainly, no one ever goes into teaching for the money, and there is little doubt that teachers do important work. However, the implication that, because of the intrinsic meaningfulness of the job, teachers will be happy, just doesn't stand up. We have already looked at data which shows senior leaders' wellbeing to be at worryingly low levels and the results of other research studies show that these concerns about wellbeing extend to teaching staff.

One survey of 3000 UK educators suggested that 77 per cent had experienced or were experiencing symptoms of poor mental health due to their work, with work-life balance and workload being cited as the most common causes of this (Education Support, 2021). Another report (Jerrim et al., 2021) provided additional insight into the drivers of workplace stress for teachers, identifying: accountability requirements, marking, changing governmental edicts, and administrative tasks as the most commonly stated reasons for anxiety and mental health problems. A third study (Kidger et al., 2016) found that, as well as workload issues being a contributory factor to teacher stress, wanting to talk to a colleague about work issues but not feeling able to, also led to high levels of dissatisfaction. This last finding has resonance with Helen Woodley and Morrison McGill's (2018) qualitative research on how 'toxic' school environments make teachers unhappy and unproductive. Woodley found that schools perceived as toxic by people who work there often display some or all of the following eight characteristics:

- high turnover of staff;
- lack of professional commitment;
- pressure-inducing micromanagement;
- mismanaged change initiatives;
- inflexible top-down structures;
- departments and groups working in isolation;

- a teaching culture of individualism;
- a negative 'groupthink' mentality among SLT members and other influential stakeholders.

All of these research studies point towards two broad themes, which seem to underpin stress experienced by teachers and may provide a threat to their wellbeing:

1 workload related to areas such as marking, planning, accountability and changing requirements and demands within the role;
2 an unsupportive school culture.

Let's look now at how coaching in schools has the potential to improve teacher wellbeing in relation to both of these areas.

We start with school culture and an idea which is central to the thesis of this book: *a coaching approach is both the product of and the driver of an authentic culture of collaboration and support.* The coaching structures and systems we have looked at are rooted in the ideas of mutual support, a universal commitment to improvement and a willingness to take professional risks and to push beyond comfort zones. These values are certainly reinforced by a coaching approach, but crucially they also need to be present in order for a coaching approach to be able to take root and thrive. Too many schools profess to offer collaborative and supportive working environments, but when it comes to it, fail to deliver on this because the actual lived attitudes and values present in the school are out of kilter with what is described. This is illustrated in the way in which some schools respond to mistakes or vulnerability shown by teachers. I have been in schools which have Growth Mindset posters around the building, celebrating the importance of embracing and learning from failure, and yet in the same school teachers feel hounded and under pressure not to admit to getting things wrong. This rarely comes about because of bad faith on the part of leaders or anyone else in the school, rather it is often born out of external pressures and accountability measures, which are in themselves punitive and unforgiving of heads.

This is not the place for a critique of inspection systems or the ways in which schools are held to account, but it is important at this point to correct a common misconception about these areas and their relation to school culture. It is often perceived that there is a degree of incompatibility between supportive, collaborative cultures and the delivery of good exam results and favourable inspection judgements. This is the notion that, in order for schools to be successful, they need to be hard-nosed, data-driven environments, where relentless accountability drives constant improvement. There are two problems with this. First, as we already saw in Chapter 3, a collaborative coaching culture can actually be linked to better learning outcomes for students. Likewise, inspectors will often recognise the positive impact of such environments, as illustrated by one English school, previously in Special Measures, which was credited by Ofsted for a rapid and sustainable turnaround, fuelled by a focus on student and staff wellbeing and ethical leadership (Uttley and Tomsett, 2020). Second, the fact that a narrow focus on school 'performance' may, and often does, have wider negative effects on the wellbeing and mental health of its community members, suggests that we may need to think differently about what 'success' actually means in a school context. If a school has high achieving results yet unhappy staff and students, can it really be seen as successful?

So, how can a coaching approach play a role in creating a supportive school culture where wellbeing is a priority for all? A good starting point for considering this is that provided by the developing field of Positive Psychology. Positive Psychology can be understood as the science of what makes us happy, standing in contrast to the focus of traditional psychology, which tends to be concerned with dysfunction. The pre-eminent figure in Positive Psychology is Martin Seligman, whose extensive research in the area led him to propose 'PERMA' (Seligman, 2013) as a model for understanding the nature of wellbeing. We will now consider each element described in this mnemonic and the extent to which a coaching approach may be seen to evoke these contributory factors to wellbeing.

P - *The experience of **P**ositive emotions, such as joy, excitement, pride and gratitude.* Although this can be considered somewhat chicken and egg (which came first, the wellbeing or the joy?), if done well, the process of coaching should provide the coachee with the opportunity to experience such emotions. An accomplished coach will encourage the coachee to reflect positively on their achievements as well as the challenges they face, thereby facilitating positive emotional responses, which may otherwise have not been experienced.

E - *Fully focused **E**ngagement in a task.* This has also been described as 'flow', 'a state in which people are so involved in an activity that nothing else seems to matter; the experience is so enjoyable that people will continue to do it even at great cost, for the sheer sake of doing it' (Csikszentmihalyi, 1990, p. 4). Flow can be experienced through activities as diverse as skiing, making a model aeroplane or playing a video game. The experience of coaching has also been widely reported as inducing a flow state in both coaches and coachees. Certainly, when one looks at what have been described as the prerequisites of being in a state of flow – focused concentration, clarity of goals, and feeling challenged but not too challenged (ibid.) – one can easily see how these can be generated through coaching.

R - *Relationships which lead one to feel supported and valued.* Clearly, an effective coach-coachee relationship will be characterised by such qualities.

M - *Being involved in activities or experiences which have significant personal Meaning because they speak to fundamental values and beliefs.* A coaching conversation aims to move beyond the superficial, seeking to help a coachee find solutions which are in line with their basic personal drivers and motivators. We have seen how EXACT coaching goals are designed to be 'powerful' and 'emotionally compelling'; in order to have these qualities, such goals will also need to be meaningful to a coachee, in that they resonate with their values and sense of personal worth.

A - *A sense of Accomplishment.* Coaching is all about striving towards meaningful goals, so it follows that the process leads to a sense of accomplishment in the coachee when these goals are successfully achieved.

We can see that all of the contributory factors to wellbeing outlined in the PERMA model have the potential to be generated by being coached. It is important to stress that here we are focusing on involvement in the *process* of coaching, which in itself seems to generate wellbeing. This is in line with much of the feedback I receive from the coachees I work with, who often say that they find the sessions energising and leave feeling more optimistic about the future.

Martin Seligman's work on 'learned optimism' is also useful in thinking about the relationship between coaching and wellbeing. At first reading, learned optimism may seem to be similar to the rather nebulous idea of positive thinking (if you think good thoughts, good things will happen). But it is, in fact, rooted in the more pragmatic idea of actively seeking pathways to positive outcomes, rather than just wishing for them: 'The basis of optimism does not lie in positive phrases or images of victory, but in the way you think about causes' (Seligman, 2018, p. 52). Research suggests that learned optimism is associated with improved health, motivation and performance, as well as career success (Moore, 2019).

Seligman's theory suggests that as well as being learned, optimism can be taught. This is where coaching comes in. Indeed, a coach using a standard facilitative approach to support a coachee to frame and feel positive about their goals will, in effect, be teaching optimism, albeit in an indirect way. However, there may be occasions when a coachee has developed negative thinking patterns, which have become engrained and are difficult to shift. In such situations, a more pro-active and direct approach to 'teaching optimism' may be required.

As we move into this territory, it is vital to stress straight away that everything that follows in this section is related to the kind of negative thinking patterns that all of us are prone to on occasions and can be considered to be within the normal range of such things. If at any time a coach has the slightest concern that a coachee with whom they are working is displaying signs of depression or any other type of mental health condition, they should not attempt to 'treat' this with coaching and instead, whenever appropriate, suggest the coachee seeks the support of a qualified therapist. It cannot be emphasised strongly enough that *coaching is not therapy*; coaches have neither the qualifications, nor the experience, to work with mental health conditions.

Having said this, a coaching approach is suitable for working with a very common phenomenon, which many of us find ourselves falling victim to on occasions, that of thinking errors or cognitive distortions. These unhelpful thinking styles tend to be negative, repeated and automatic, and crucially are not reflective of reality. When we experience them, they tend to run counter to any sort of optimism we may aspire to and are therefore problematic when we are trying to set motivating goals. Ten common types of cognitive distortion have been identified (Burns, 1981), and these are listed below with illustrative examples related to things which may be said as part of a coaching conversation:

1 All or nothing thinking (thinking that one has either very positive or very negative personal qualities): '*I'll never be able to do that, I'm afraid I'm just too impatient!*'

2 Over-generalisation (thinking that because something happened once, it will happen again and again): '*I tried that out in my class last week, it went awfully, I'm not going to try it again, it's bound to go wrong.*'

3 Mental filter (thinking that focuses on a negative element and dwells on this, thereby making the whole picture appear negative): '*I know the training session didn't go well, I saw my deputy looking out of the window for most of it, she was bored out of her mind.*'

4 Disqualifying the positive (thinking that regards something positive as having happened as an anomaly or by chance): '*Yes, the lesson went well but it was only because you were in there observing; if you hadn't been there, it would have been a disaster.*'

5 Mind reading (thinking that assumes someone else is thinking badly of you): *'I don't want to ask her for help, she thinks I'm useless already.'*

6 Magnification and minimisation (thinking that exaggerates errors or problems and sees achievements or strengths as unimportant): *'It doesn't matter that I achieved one part of the goal, look at all the stuff I didn't manage to do, what a mess!'*

7 Emotional reasoning (thinking that comprehends something though emotions being experienced, rather than what is actually happening): *'I felt so nervous during the presentation, it went terribly.'*

8 Should statements (thinking that can be intended to motivate oneself, but which can generate feelings of guilt or shame): *'As I was talking to her, I felt my voice go wobbly. I kept thinking to myself, I really should be able to say this. It's pathetic.'*

9 Labelling (thinking that rigidly assigns a certain characteristic to oneself): *'I really can't bring myself to go to that networking event. I'm just not a people person.'*

10 Personalisation (thinking that assigns blame to oneself, despite this not being the case): *'But I'm in charge. If it goes wrong, it's my fault and my fault only.'*

The last cognitive distortion type listed here was one I was particularly prone to during my own career as a school leader. The example given is typical of the type of thinking that would go on in my head, if an event, initiative or plan did not go well. In retrospect, I can see that many such situations were in fact caused by factors I had no control over; but this is not the story I told myself at the time.

Cognitive distortions are particularly problematic because of the fact that they tend to become engrained over time. This can be explained by neuroscience: we know that every time we repeat an action or thought, the neural pathways in our brain that govern this thought or action become deeper and deeper, meaning that eventually they are so well established that the action or thought becomes automatic. Think of driving; when learning to drive initially we use significant cognitive resources in order to master the various combinations of actions needed to carry out the task; but having done so the process quickly becomes automatic, to the extent that we can sometimes find ourselves at a destination without remembering the drive there! We will delve deeper into cognitive science and its implications for coaching in Chapter 5, but for now we can use what we know about how cognitive distortions become habitual to think about how coaching can help coachees to undo such unhelpful thinking patterns.

In line with standard coaching theory, a coach is likely to meet with little success by simply telling a coachee that their thoughts are incorrect. Rather, an approach which encourages the coachee to reflect on and question their thought patterns themselves is likely to have more impact. One way to do this is through Socratic questioning.

The Greek philosopher Socrates was said to have developed this technique to enable his students to examine the validity of their ideas. To do this, he adopted a position of ignorance about what was being discussed and used a series of open-ended questions designed to allow his students to get to the 'truth' of the topic, rather than offering his own ideas. The similarities with modern coaching methodology are clear. Richard Paul's (Paul and Elder, 2016) taxonomy of Socratic questions is a good place to start when thinking about how the approach can be used to coach cognitive distortions. Table 4.1 summarises the question types in this model, and using some of the examples of faulty thinking outlined above, suggests some questions that may be asked to move a coachee forward.

Of course, correcting cognitive distortions will not be achieved through the asking of a single question. As with any type of coaching, how questions are selected, how they are linked and how they build on what has previously been said will be key in deciding how successful the process is. A coach should ideally seek to draw on these question types but guard against falling into a systematic tick-box approach to using them.

Likewise, long held cognitive distortions will not be shifted by a single coaching session, or even through a series of sessions. In order for changes to occur, coachees will need to become alert to cognitive distortions they are prone to, noticing them when they occur and literally practising thinking differently in order to develop new neural pathways. The coach may then provide a space for ongoing reflection, which should reinforce and focus the ongoing work being done by the coachee.

So far, we have concentrated on how coaching can contribute to a supportive school culture which promotes wellbeing, by proactively providing happiness-inducing experiences and by providing a space for tackling negative thinking. We now move on to thinking about the issue of workload and pressures related to accountability, and ask the question, how can coaching provide support to teachers and leaders in these areas?

Obviously, what a coaching approach cannot do is remove these barriers to wellbeing. Shifting requirements and priorities in schools, on macro or micro levels, may increase or decrease pressures over time, but in reality workload and accountability systems will always have some sort of impact on the stress levels of teachers and school leaders.

Table 4.1 Socratic questioning and cognitive distortions

Question type	Example of cognitive distortion	Example Socratic question
Clarification	'I'll never be able to do that, I'm afraid I'm just too impatient!'	What do you mean when you say I'm just too impatient?
Challenging assumptions	'Yes, the lesson went well but it was only because you were in there observing; if you hadn't been there, it would have been a disaster.'	Are you saying that is the only thing that helped? What other things may have contributed to the lesson going well?
Evidence and reasoning	'I don't want to ask her for help, she thinks I'm useless already.'	Can you provide an example that shows she thinks you're useless?
Alternative viewpoints	'But I'm in charge. If it goes wrong, it's my fault and my fault only.'	What other ways of thinking about this are there?
Implications and consequences	'As I was talking to her, I felt my voice go wobbly. I kept thinking to myself, I really should be able to say this. It's pathetic.'	What effect is this type of thinking having on you? What impact is it having on your ability to achieve your goals?

Figure 4.1 Mind Manager

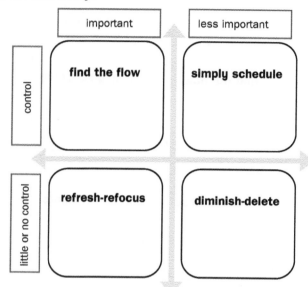

Having said this, what a coaching approach can do is provide a space for gaining perspective on these issues and for considering practical strategies which may reduce the impact they have on wellbeing. Figure 4.1 is a description of the Mind Manager, a simple tool I have developed to support my coachees in this area.

Combining ideas from two models developed by Stephen Covey (Control, Influence and Concern Circles, and the Eisenhower Matrix) (Covey, 1989), the Mind Manager provides a method for reflecting on how we make use of our finite cognitive capacity at work. Standing in contrast to traditional time-management tools, which tend to be focused on tasks, it takes into account the fact that, while we often use our mental energies in a focused and productive way, we can also spend time worrying, procrastinating and pontificating about things which are not important, or over which we have little or no control.

I tend to introduce the model by inviting my coachee to brainstorm all the work-related matters that are on their mind at that time. The idea is that the list is as comprehensive as possible and should include 'big things' as well as 'little things'. We then set about categorising these, by placing them in one of the quadrants on the Mind Manager, depending on their level of importance and the degree of control the coachee has over the matter. As often is

Figure 4.2 Mind Manager with examples

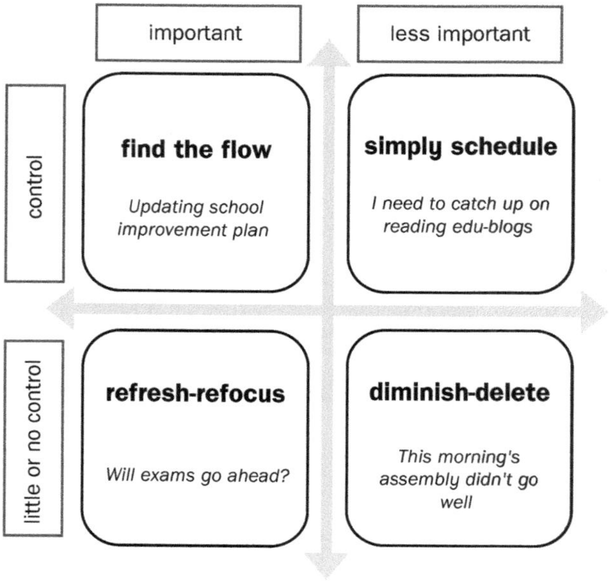

	important	less important
control	**find the flow** *Updating school improvement plan*	**simply schedule** *I need to catch up on reading edu-blogs*
little or no control	**refresh-refocus** *Will exams go ahead?*	**diminish-delete** *This morning's assembly didn't go well*

the case with this type of exercise, the discussion that is involved in this, is as important as the outcomes. Some examples of things that may come up are shown in Figure 4.2.

We then move on to the 'managing' part of the exercise. At this stage, based on where the different matters have been placed on the quadrant, the coachee is encouraged to carry out one of the following:

1 *Diminish-delete* (for matters which are less important and over which the coachee has little or no control). Cognitive resources used on such things are wasted cognitive resources. Although this may appear obvious, we still sometimes have a tendency to dwell on the unimportant and the uncontrollable. The mental exercise of examining and recognising the lack of importance of and control we have over these matters is the first step to consciously deciding to stop or reduce expending cognitive energy on them.

2 *Simply schedule* (for matters which are less important but over which the coachee has a degree of control). Research indicates that the very act of scheduling something which is creating worry or using mental energy, allows us to stop thinking about it (McGowan and Behar, 2013).

3 *Refresh-refocus* (for matters which are important but over which the coachee has little or no control). Whether it be world peace, or the cost of living, we all often find ourselves thinking or worrying about important things, which we have no influence over. This is as much the case for issues related to our professional lives as it is more widely. Clearly it is not realistic to simply decide to switch off from such things, so when our mental resources are being depleted in such a way, it can often be a good strategy to engage in a relaxation exercise, such as meditation or deep breathing, before then refocusing, ideally on matters which fall into the final category ...

4 *Find the flow* (for matters which are important and over which the coachee has a degree of control). This is the 'golden quadrant', containing matters on which coachees should be focusing the majority of their cognitive resources. The best way to achieve this is to aspire to a state of 'flow', where one is immersed and fully focused on what is being done. We have already touched on this idea of flow in relation to what makes us happy, but what is the best way to attain this state? A summary of research in this area (Cherry, 2020) suggests the following factors are key: skills are stretched but not over-stretched; clear goals are present; interruptions are minimised; and a focus on the process itself. In addition, a reduction in mental energies expended on unimportant matters, or those beyond our control as described above, will in itself provide a context in which flow is more likely to occur.

We have seen that coaching can certainly support education professionals in managing the stresses and strains of their work. However, in order to have a sustainable impact, the focus of such coaching has to be on helping coachees move away from support and towards independence in managing their own wellbeing. Key to this, is the concept of practice. All of the techniques and approaches discussed in this chapter relate in some way to developing new habits of the mind. In order to ensure these different ways of thinking become engrained, a coachee will need to practise them. Such practice is needed in order for changes in the brain to occur, which brings us to the focus of our next chapter.

5 Coaching and the brain

As each year goes by, we are understanding more and more about the cognitive processes involved in learning and this is increasingly being reflected in instructional design in schools. Much of what we are finding out about the brain, and its implications for pedagogy, also has pertinence to andragogy and professional learning.

In this chapter we take some neuro and cognitive science ideas and concepts commonly applied in the classroom, and explore how they are also useful for providing insight into how coaching works and best practice in this area.

Deliberate practice

In working towards mastery of their craft, teachers and leaders benefit from engaging in deliberate practice in order to facilitate changes in long-term memory.

What is learning? When this question is asked in educational circles, there can sometimes be a tendency to conflate nature with purpose and to be side-tracked by musings about why we educate and the function of schooling. But rather than a philosophical question, this is a biological one. The following statement has gained great currency as a way of understanding learning in recent years: 'If nothing has changed in long-term memory, nothing has been learned' (Kirschner et al., 2006, p. 77). This concept of learning as a change in the state of the brain is a useful one, as it leaves aside questions of application and transference (which are important but separate notions), and leaves us with a simple idea of learning being about knowing something new and retaining that knowledge over an extended period of time.

Cognitive scientists distinguish between two types of knowledge: procedural knowledge, or 'knowing how', and declarative knowledge, or 'knowing what'. A teacher or school leader's declarative knowledge may include knowing: what Vygotsky's theory of proximal development is, the details of the school behaviour policy, and the contents of the current Ofsted inspection framework. On the other hand, their procedural knowledge may include: knowing how to use a visualiser, knowing how to deliver different questioning routines in the classroom, and knowing how to deploy strategies for handling difficult conversations.

Coaching will usually be focused on developing a teacher's or leader's procedural as opposed to declarative knowledge. According to the definition of learning referenced above, a successful coaching intervention should lead to changes in a coachee's long-term memory related to the procedural knowledge being focused on, which in turn will lead to increasing automaticity in the coachee's deployment of this procedural knowledge. So, for example, the success of a teacher coaching process focused on questioning routines will be defined by the coachee's ability to confidently, and with reducing conscious effort, decide when and how to deploy these routines.

Many psychologists believe procedural knowledge is best developed through 'deliberate practice'. This term was coined by Anders Ericsson, who defined deliberate practice as 'a highly structured activity, the explicit goal of which is to improve performance' (Ericsson et al., 1993, p. 368). Ericsson's theory was that repeated practice in a highly focused area, where planning for improvement and reflection are built into the process, will lead to mastery. Thus, in the sporting world, an example of deliberate practice would be a tennis player spending hours on their serve, seeking feedback and making adjustments accordingly, rather than just playing practice sets. Although tennis is mainly a physical activity as opposed to a cerebral one, the effects of deliberate practice, whether they be in relation to a sport, study or professional activity, are neurological in nature. The more procedural knowledge is applied through practice, the stronger associated neural pathways become, and as a result, the more automatic the process becomes. Interestingly, brain studies (Australian Academy of Science, 2018) have also shown that novices demonstrate widespread activity in areas of the brain related to controlled planning while engaging in deliberate practice, while experts show significantly reduced activity in these areas when doing the same activities; it is suggested that this 'freed up' capacity accounts for experts' ability to make quick efficient decisions.

Deans for Impact, a US teacher preparation organisation, has produced an excellent document, which defines five principles of deliberate practice and explores their implications for the development of trainee and early career teachers. These five principles are:

1 Move out of one's comfort zone.
2 Work towards specific goals.

3 Maintain a tight focus on practice activities.
4 Receive and act on feedback.
5 Work towards a mental model of expertise.

(Deans for Impact, 2016)

Deans for Impact's work was focused on deliberate practice in all forms of professional development with particular regard to novice teachers. However these principles apply particularly well to the specific area of PD through coaching.

1 Move out of one's comfort zone

A 'comfort zone' has been described as 'a behavioural state within which a person operates in an anxiety-neutral condition, using a limited set of behaviours to deliver a steady level of performance, usually without a sense of risk' (White, 2008, p. 2). Thus, being in a comfort zone provides a sense of safety and of being in control but also tends to inhibit growth. Whether a coach is working with a teacher to help them develop their classroom practice and impact on learning, or with a leader to support them in overcoming challenges or becoming more effective in their role, the safe space provided by the coaching process is ideal for coaxing coachees out of their comfort zones. It is very possible that the process of establishing stretching goals will engender anxiety in coachees, and here again, the highly supportive environment of a coaching relationship is crucial in helping coachees to manage this.

2 Work towards specific goals

All coaching models place the establishment of focused and measurable goals at the centre of the process and therefore coaching is clearly in line with this principle of deliberate practice.

3 Maintain a tight focus on practice activities

Deans for Impact reference two mechanisms for this type of focused practice: decompositions and approximations (Grossman et al., 2009). Although these were conceived of specifically in relation to teaching practice, they are useful when thinking about the types of practice that either teacher or school leader coachees may engage in. A decomposition is the isolation of one specific practice among a complex range of practices. In line with this, leadership and teaching models of coaching have in common the identification of and focus on specified priorities. Approximation, on the other hand, refers to the imitation of a practice and can be seen in teacher coaching models, which may include rehearsal or modelling of a strategy. Whilst this mechanism is less commonly used in leadership coaching, there may be opportunities for sessions to include approximation of situations, such as difficult conversations, presentations or job interviews.

4 Receive and act on feedback

Again, to a greater or lesser degree, all teacher coaching models will include feedback as a part of the process. We have seen that some models place emphasis on facilitated reflection but some sort of feedback from a coach is always likely to feature in teacher coaching. Similarly, teacher coaching models are structured in such a way as to allow the coachee to make adjustments based on feedback. Leadership coaching models rarely involve observation of practice, with facilitated 'self-feedback' likely to be used instead of direct feedback from the coach.

5 Work towards a mental model of expertise

A mental model has been defined as 'the knowledge held by an individual and the way it is organised to guide action' (Barker and Rees, 2020). In line with this, the aim of coaching is to help the coachee develop procedural knowledge and crucially to become increasingly aware of how and when to best apply this knowledge in order to achieve goals or overcome challenges.

Retrieval practice

Recall or retrieval of prior professional learning and knowledge is essential for retention in long-term memory. Put simply, retrieval practice is the calling to mind of previous learning. Research shows that the very act of retrieving knowledge, be this procedural or declarative, has the effect of improving our 'grasp' of that knowledge. Indeed, thanks to the work of Hermann Ebbinghaus (1885) we have known this for more than a hundred years. Ebbinghaus conducted experiments which showed that memory of learned materials decays over time unless that learning is reviewed repeatedly. Now, due to developments in cognitive science, we understand that this happens because neural pathways associated with the knowledge being retrieved are strengthened as we undertake the mental exercise of recalling.

Retrieval practice is increasingly becoming a staple of pedagogy, and there are many teaching resources available which are designed to facilitate recall in students, thereby improving their learning. The principles of retrieval practice in the classroom can also be applied to professional learning, and are particularly useful when thinking about making a connection between 'traditional' forms of CPD and a coaching approach.

As already stated, this book does not set out to suggest that coaching should completely replace forms of professional learning such as courses, conferences and workshops; rather, that carefully designed and intentionally planned professional development programmes should include many forms of CPD, including coaching. The cumulative impact of these differing elements will be governed by the extent to which they link logically together, while providing for the particular needs of a school and its professionals. One way of understanding the way that coaching and other forms of CPD can combine, is to make a parallel with the relationship between content teaching and retrieval practice in the classroom. If we see teacher attendance at training sessions, conferences or workshops as being the equivalent of a student being taught new skills, ideas and knowledge in the classroom, we can regard coaching as an opportunity for recall and application of this content, which is equivalent to effective lesson sequences that include meaningful retrieval opportunities. Coaching which is more directive in nature (which, as we have seen, is most usefully used with novices), may include both 'content teaching' and 'retrieval practice'. One-to-one coaching has the additional benefit of allowing the retrieval and application of knowledge to be applied in a personalised way, which responds to the particular needs and priorities of the coachee.

An example of this might be a teacher who identifies that low-level disruption is negatively impacting learning in their class and decides to attend a training day focused on behaviour for learning. The teacher leaves the course having heard about a number of strategies and routines, which they are keen to try out. In many cases, such a teacher will get back to the hurly-burly of the classroom and simply forget, not only many of the strategies taught, but also the enthusiasm they had felt at the end of the course. Because of the demands of the job, they do not actively engage in the recall and reflection required for learning to take place. On the other hand, if the teacher has access to coaching, a formalised 'space' for recall and reflection is provided. As a result, the teacher is then able to use these sessions to enter into a cycle of retrieving, reflecting, planning and implementing, thereby ensuring they are creating the best conditions for meaningful and useful learning to take place.

Desirable difficulty

Challenge in professional learning needs to be framed by the concept of 'desirable difficulty'. The term 'desirable difficulty' was coined by Robert Bjork (1994) and is a refinement of the concept of retrieval practice. Bjork's studies suggested that activities designed to facilitate the retrieval and/or application of content or concepts previously introduced, need to hit a 'sweet spot' of being neither too challenging nor too easy for the person doing the retrieving/applying. Approaches which are lacking in challenge may lead the learner to believe they have deeply 'learned' something, when in reality they may only have done so in a superficial way. On the other hand, if a task is too challenging, for example if it requires the learner to draw extensively on knowledge they do not have, they are likely to become frustrated and to give up. Professor Rob Coe famously said 'learning happens when people have to think hard' (2013, p. 13) and although this may at first appear simplistic, it is in line with Bjork's findings that struggle is an important part of learning.

The concept of desirable difficulties has clear applicability in the context of coaching. A coach using a question-based approach to support a coachee is consciously facilitating meaningful mental struggle. By avoiding immediately 'telling' a coachee what to do and rather asking questions which require them to draw on previous experience or knowledge in order to make sense of a situation or to make plans for moving forward, a coach is creating desirable difficulty.

Cognitive load theory (CLT)

In order to avoid overload of working memory, teachers and leaders will benefit from ensuring development areas are tightly focused. Cognitive load theory (CLT) is another area of psychology which is having an increasing influence on teaching and instructional design. The basic idea of this theory is that our brain's information processing capabilities are linked to two components:

1 working memory, which is the site of conscious thinking or processing;
2 long-term memory, which is where knowledge is stored.

CLT suggests that our working memory is finite in capacity and as a result of this is subject to overload if required to process more than five to seven items of information at any one time. This clearly has implications for teaching. As John Sweller, the author of the theory, put it: 'Anything beyond the simplest cognitive activities appear to overwhelm working memory. Prima facie, any instructional design that flouts or merely ignores working memory limitations inevitably is deficient' (Sweller et al., 1998, p. 252).

In the classroom, an application of CLT leads teachers to give thought to not overloading their students' working memories by presenting too much information at once, and avoiding unnecessary or extraneous information not linked to the learning focus. Similarly, coaches working in schools would do well to consider CLT in their own practice. Specifically, it is important to recognise that coachees are likely to find it challenging to deal with multiple concepts and ideas in any one session. The structured and highly focused nature of most coaching models helps to facilitate this but coaches should still guard against wide-ranging 'roller-coaster' sessions, which leave the coachee feeling exhausted and possibly confused. Slow-paced, focused and deliberative approaches to coaching tend to be successful exactly because they take into account the limited capacity of working memory.

Another aspect of CLT pertinent to coaches is the idea that limitations on working memory are reduced when someone is able to relate new information to information already stored in their long-term memory. The introduction of novel concepts through reference to pre-existing knowledge seems to have the effect of anchoring this new information and reducing the stress on the working memory. This implies that good practice in coaching will include the signposting of relevant connected previous knowledge when tackling new ideas or concepts.

The Expertise Reversal Effect

The Expertise Reversal Effect needs to be considered in ensuring varying levels of prior knowledge and experience are taken into account when coaching. We have seen how structured guidance and scaffolding are essential for novice learners lacking well-developed schemas (frameworks of knowledge) in order to ensure they do not become cognitively overloaded by new ideas and information. However, interestingly some studies suggest that if such approaches are used with more expert learners who already have well-developed schemas, they can have the effect of creating unproductive cognitive load through the presentation of 'redundant' information. This Expertise Reversal Effect was identified by a group of researchers who explained the theory by stating that, 'unless experienced learners can avoid processing redundant units of information, they must integrate and cross-reference this redundant information with their available knowledge schemas. This activity can place an excessive and unnecessary load on limited working memory resources' (Kalyuga et al., 2011, p. 29). Therefore, in effect, scaffolding and structure, designed to support novice learners, can actually have a negative effect on expert learners because their cognitive resources are depleted by focusing on things which are actually unnecessary to them as learners.

The Expertise Reversal Effect provides an interesting new perspective on the discussion earlier in this book about differing types of coaching approaches used in schools and when they may or may not be appropriate to deploy. It suggests that if more structured approaches to coaching are applied with teachers or leaders who have a pre-existing degree of knowledge and expertise, then a focus on process and transmission may undermine the coachee's ability to engage meaningfully with the process because it will lead to a 'misuse' of their cognitive capacity. Rather, coachees with a level of expertise will benefit from deploying their mental energies on the reflection and joint problem-solving offered by dialogic models of coaching. The Expertise Reversal Effect further emphasises the importance of schools being intentional and careful in their deployment of differing approaches to coaching.

Trusting relationships

Cognitive science confirms that positive and trusting relationships underpin impactful coaching. We have already explored the importance of trust in coaching and the need for coachees to feel they are in a 'psychologically safe' space in order for the experience to be worthwhile. We will now look at the neuroscientific underpinnings of this.

Scientists have identified evidence which indicates that our brains are hard-wired to seek out positive relationships (Tomova et al., 2020). These findings suggest that cravings for connection are located in the same area of the brain as food cravings, while feelings of loneliness are experienced in the region of the brain where physical pain is experienced. Conversely, positive interactions trigger a number of responses in the brain which are conducive to reflection and learning (Kaufman, 2021):

1 release of dopamine, the pleasure hormone;
2 release of oxytocin, the bonding hormone, often associated with a feeling of psychological safety;

3 inhibit release of cortisol, the stress hormone;

4 free up working memory from anxieties and misgivings, providing greater cognitive capacity for meaningful reflection and learning.

All of this provides scientific credence to what many of us intuitively hold to be true: that coaching is unlikely to be successful if it is not underpinned by emotional intelligence, empathy and authenticity on the part of both coach and coachee.

Summary

Increasingly, our understanding of how and why coaching works is being informed by the developing areas of cognitive science and neuroscience. Indeed, 'neurocoaching' is a new multi-disciplinary approach which encompasses many of the ideas touched on in this chapter. As one of the major proponents of this emerging approach puts it, neurocoaching adds value to the field of coaching because 'firstly, it enables high levels of neurological engagement during coaching sessions, and secondly it enables sustainable change through self-directed neuroplasticity' (Bosman, 2021). For both these reasons, coaches in educational settings should always seek to keep abreast of ongoing developments in brain science, not only to ensure that their practice is having the maximum positive impact on their coachees, but also so they can pass on to their coachees neuroscientific insights which will benefit both their self-directed learning and their teaching in the classroom.

6 Building and sustaining a culture of coaching

Over the years, many people have grappled with the complexity of organisational culture as a concept and have attempted to offer simple, accessible definitions. Among all of these, the one that resonates most with me was contributed as part of a LinkedIn discussion thread on the topic by KPMG Executive, Richard Perrin: 'Organizational culture is the sum of values and rituals which serve as "glue" to integrate the members of the organization' (Watkins, 2013). This definition tallies with the work of Edgar Schein (1985), who described three levels of culture:

1 *Artefacts and symbols*: the most visible characteristics of organisational culture such as policies, processes, logos, slogans and observable actions.
2 *Espoused values and beliefs*: the organisation's approach and expectations – 'how things are done here'.
3 *Underlying assumptions*: what the people, who make up a culture, actually believe.

The metaphor of an iceberg is often associated with Schein's levels of culture, with 'artefacts and symbols' being the most visible part of the iceberg above the waterline (in oceanographic terms, this is known as the hummock); 'espoused values and beliefs' being the section just under the surface of the water (this is the upper part of what is called the bummock); and 'underlying assumptions' being symbolised by the bottom part of the iceberg (the lower section of the bummock), monolithic but largely invisible.

This chapter will use the iceberg metaphor (Figure 6.1) to examine the elements which I think are essential in the creation of a school culture of coaching.

Figure 6.1 Elements of a school culture of coaching

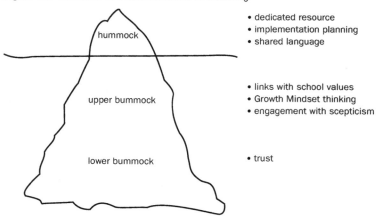

- dedicated resource
- implementation planning
- shared language

- links with school values
- Growth Mindset thinking
- engagement with scepticism

- trust

The hummock

Dedicated resource (time and money)

Schools committed to placing coaching at the heart of professional development will need to take some very practical steps in order to realise this ambition. Not least among these is the dedication of time and money to the project.

Taking a coaching approach to CPD in schools is probably more expensive in temporal terms than it is in financial terms. Protected time is necessary for coaching sessions to take place, and additional time may be needed for coaches to carry out observations (although the use of video can reduce this load).

As anyone who has worked in one knows, time is just about the most precious resource there is in a school; there simply never is enough of it. This means that a decision to implement coaching cannot afford to involve just layering the approach on top of everything else that is happening in the school. If there is one sure-fire way of making a coaching project crash and burn, this is it. Schools will need to engage in the difficult process of finding time for sessions to happen and this will almost inevitably involve doing less of something else. If a school comes to the conclusion that there is nothing else that can go or be modified in order to make time and space for quality coaching to take place, questions would need to be asked about whether the school is really ready or committed enough to gain full benefit from the approach.

Many schools have found the time to introduce coaching by thinking differently about observations and meetings that are already happening.

Teacher observations for the purposes of quality assurance and accountability have long been a staple of school life around the world. However, as well as being a stressful experience for all involved, it has been argued that such an approach to making judgements about the quality of a teacher's work is fundamentally flawed for various reasons:

1 It has been shown that different observers often have completely different views about the 'quality' of an observed lesson (Bill and Melinda Gates Foundation, 2013).

2 It is impossible to gauge whether/how much students are learning by observing a single lesson.

3 Student 'engagement', which is often identified as an important area for observers to focus on, is in fact a poor proxy for learning.

4 There is a strong possibility that observers will not witness 'normal practice', due to the observed teacher behaving differently.

5 The range of data that many schools require observers to collect in a single session is often so wide that it is almost impossible to carry out meaningful or useful observations.

For all of these reasons, an increasing number of schools are making the decision to change the purpose and nature of classroom observations, so that instead of being focused on evaluating or judging teacher effectiveness, they become part of a developmental teacher coaching programme.

Similarly, many schools have managed to create space for coaching conversations by taking time from regular scheduled meetings. By making meetings more efficient or by doing away altogether with those that have the purpose of passing on information which could be passed on in a different way, these schools demonstrate their commitment to making collaboration and collective development the default reason for professional interactions.

The main direct financial costs involved in implementing a coaching approach to professional development revolve around building professional capacity. In order to develop confidence and competence in the skills and approaches of coaching, schools will ideally design a programme which draws on traditional training models as well as 'coaching about coaching sessions' to build professional capacity over time. Some schools identify Coaching Champions, who have the role of co-ordinating and leading such programmes.

An additional financial cost may come from paying for external coaches to work with certain members of staff (often, but not exclusively, those in senior leadership positions). Indeed, this is something I support schools with, and I find that leaders regard external coaching as a cost-effective and motivating way to develop their practice.

Implementation planning

As well as investing sufficient time and money in coaching programmes, schools wishing to embark on such initiatives will also need to ensure that they plan carefully for the roll-out. At this stage, it is useful to highlight a report published by the Education Endowment Foundation (EEF), which provides 'implementation guidance' for schools (Education Endowment Foundation, 2019): a set of recommendations of best practice in rolling out school improvement/development initiatives. This report outlines two 'foundations' for good implementation and four 'stages', or 'steps', of effective implementation. We will take each of these in turn and explore how they could be applied in relation to the implementation of a coaching approach to professional development in a school.

Foundation 1: 'Treat implementation as a process, not an event; plan and execute it in stages' (p. 8)

The implementation of a coaching-based approach to professional development will always be a challenging and complicated project for any school. Some schools I know of have decided the best approach for them was to move quickly to rolling out a comprehensive programme across the school; others have 'started small' with pilot projects, followed by an incremental roll-out. Both approaches are appropriate, but only if they are planned for in a structured and staged manner. The EEF report states that it can take between two and four years to implement complex initiatives and I would suggest that implementing a coaching approach certainly falls into that category. Schools need to be realistic and pragmatic in their implementation planning and be prepared for 'bumps in the road', which may change and extend timelines.

Foundation 2: 'Create a leadership environment and school climate that is conducive to good implementation' (p. 10)

Given the vital importance of leadership and climate for an initiative such as coaching, steeped as it is in enabling and trusting relationships, I see this as the most fundamental of the EEF's six recommendations. I will explore this in detail when we come to the lower bummock, the largest part of the cultural iceberg, which gives ballast to the rest of the structure.

Step 1 Explore: 'Define the problem you want to solve and identify appropriate programmes or practices to implement' (p. 12)

The immediate question this first step to effective implementation begs is, why might a school consider introducing a coaching approach to CPD? To be frank, in some cases, the answer may be, 'because everyone else seems to be doing it'. There is a strong possibility that as it becomes more known about, coaching in schools will suffer from the kind of bandwagon jumping that many other educational 'trends' have been prone to over the years. I use the word 'suffer' advisedly because there is a substantial risk that if schools decide to take on coaching without fully understanding what is involved, or considering why and how it will help them achieve their priorities, the project will fail. In such scenarios, another possibility is that a 'lethal mutation' will occur, whereby an approach delivered under the label of coaching manifests as something completely different and possibly counterproductive. I have seen examples of schools that deliver high stakes teacher observation and feedback programmes, which are called coaching but which, in reality, have very little in common with the approach.

Schools will ideally have identified coaching as something they would like to develop, as a result of it potentially offering a solution to a 'problem' they have defined or as an avenue to improvement in a certain area. These may include issues as different as: teacher retention, student behaviour, and measurable lack of impact of other approaches to PD, among many others.

Having identified a problem/improvement priority, amenable to change through coaching, a school will then need to move to a consideration of which approach to coaching is best suited to their particular context. We have already seen that there are a range of dimensions and styles of coaching that manifest in schools, and at this stage schools would be well advised to carry out a thorough exploration of approaches available and then look to adopt or adapt the approaches that best match their needs and priorities. A study of two schools in Canada and England implementing a coaching approach to PD (Hollweck and Lofthouse, 2021) provides further evidence of the importance of schools placing their own particular context at the heart of deciding how they will design and deliver such a programme. Having looked and compared the approaches of the two schools studied, the authors concluded, 'there is no one right way to do coaching in education; it can be initiated externally or internally, but a deliberate and iterative design and structure attuned to the setting and contributing to the context is critical' (p. 413).

Step 2 Prepare: 'Create a clear implementation plan, judge the readiness of the school to deliver that plan, then prepare staff and resources' (p. 20)

The EEF report makes it clear that this stage is not just about making a plan in preparation for delivery. Rather, the authors advocate an agile approach to planning, with an ongoing focus on assessing school readiness and making adaptations to planning based on this. In the case of implementing a coaching approach, this is likely to involve asking questions such as: How motivated are the staff to participate in coaching? What level of skills related to coaching/understanding of coaching do the staff have? Do we have enough flexibility in the school calendar and timetable to make any necessary changes? If the answers to these questions suggest a change is needed in the plan, then this will need to happen before the project is taken forward.

Another important part of preparing for the launch of any initiative is communication with stakeholders. The EEF report suggests that school leaders need to clearly communicate to all staff what will be 'expected', 'supported' and 'rewarded' during implementation. Although I believe clarity of communication is essential whenever any kind of initiative is introduced, I do have some reservations about whether the language employed here in the EEF report is useful for thinking about the implementation of a coaching approach. Creating wide buy-in is certainly important (we will look at this in greater depth later in the chapter, when we consider engagement with scepticism and change management models); however, the nature of coaching means that schools should ideally seek to build this buy-in through the fostering of an intrinsic motivation to participate, based on the benefits that will be received through being coached and coaching others. Notions such as 'expectations' and 'rewards' suggest a behaviourist approach to implementation, which jars somewhat with the nature of coaching, concerned as it is with fostering change through deliberation and personal motivation, rather than top-down imposition.

Other parts of this EEF recommendation, however, are certainly useful when thinking about planning for the implementation of a coaching approach. There is an emphasis on making clear to all stakeholders how an initiative aligns with the school's purpose and current priorities, as well as stressing the importance of ensuring everyone understands what is involved in the whole process of implementation. This communication of the 'why' and 'how' is very important in helping stakeholders feel involved in the process of implementation.

Step 3 Deliver: 'Support staff, monitor progress, solve problems, and adapt strategies as the approach is used for the first time' (p. 32)

The EEF guidance uses the metaphor of gardening to help explain the process of implementation. In this metaphor, the project being implemented is a new plant being introduced to a garden; at the 'deliver' stage, this seedling is at its most vulnerable and in need of sustained care and attention to ensure its survival. In the case of the implementation of a coaching programme, this careful nurturing is likely to involve:

- sustained training in coaching techniques, with opportunities for collaboration and reflection;
- monitoring/overseeing of the way coaching is being implemented to ensure fidelity with aims and design;
- use of data to monitor the impact of the programme;
- alertness to challenges arising and willingness to respond appropriately;
- introduction of necessary adaptations (for example, style of coaching being used, timings of sessions, people involved).

Step 4 Sustain: 'Plan for sustaining and scaling an intervention from the outset and continuously acknowledge and nurture its use' (p. 38)

Schools will ideally have an 'end goal' in mind when they embark on a coaching project. This may range from a vision of informal coaching approaches underpinning conversations in a particular department, to a whole school programme of regularly scheduled formal coaching sessions. Whatever the end goal, schools do need to have one, and to communicate it to stakeholders. Mary Lippett's (1987) exploration of unsuccessful and successful complex change initiatives in institutions identified that an absence of or failure to communicate the vision for a project usually leads to confusion in stakeholders and, consequently, failure. This is not to say that a vision or end goal should not change as a project evolves. Indeed, effective implementation processes will often result in exactly this happening, as schools recalibrate projects because, for example, they see new possibilities emerging, or because unforeseen factors are having an effect on roll-out. An agile approach, accompanied by ongoing communication, is paramount here.

Another factor to take into account in planning for the scaling and sustaining of an initiative is the role of individuals. Enthusiasts and champions are very important in the initiation and driving of coaching programmes in their early stages; but equally important is the need for schools to future-proof such projects through succession planning and ensuring that the moving on of a particular person or persons does not lead to the programme collapsing. This can be done through the nurturing of new and future champions but also through intentional planning to 'normalise' the routines that frame coaching programmes. In a way that parallels deliberate practice leading to automaticity of skills and developing expertise in an individual, the embedding of effective and enabling coaching systems in a school leads to a kind of 'institutional learning' which means that the programme is not reliant on individuals to thrive.

Shared language

We have already touched on the confusion that sometimes surrounds the language of coaching. Differences in understandings of terminology within institutions can be problematic in terms of implementation, as groups and individuals put into practice their own varying interpretations of what coaching is and what it entails. These inconsistencies of approach may undermine fidelity to the original programme design, limit its impact, and sometimes generate the types of misunderstandings that lead to failure.

For these reasons, it is very important that schools spend time consciously fostering a shared language of coaching. This will mean agreeing on their own understanding of terms such as 'instructional coaching', 'mentoring', 'active listening', and other language widely used in coaching circles. Schools may even choose to create their own terminology, which reflects their particular priorities and contexts; what is important is that everyone is 'singing from the same hymn sheet' and avoiding crossed purposes when talking about coaching.

The importance of terminology related to areas of practice being used widely and consistently across a school, and understood by all stakeholders, is not solely about avoidance of problems, though. Indeed, research suggests that the prevalence of 'sticky language' related to a programme or approach is strongly correlated with positive impact generated (Grenville-Giddings, 2021). In line with this, there are numerous educational programmes and interventions available to schools which place great emphasis on the importance of shared language. I myself have been involved in two of these, the oracy programmes of Voice 21 and the Skills Builder Partnership's Universal Framework of Essential Skills. My experience working with both of these organisations has provided me with plentiful evidence of the power of shared language in educational interventions. Similarly, schools that successfully build cultures of coaching harness the power of sticky language to build understanding and commitment to a common, universally known, cause.

The upper bummock

We now head below the surface of the water to examine the 'upper bummock' of the school cultural iceberg and the elements here that will play a role in deciding how effective and impactful a school coaching programme is.

While less tangible than the artefacts and symbols of the hummock, the factors contained within the upper bummock are crucial in providing substance and ballast to any change programme in a school.

Links with school values

As we have discussed earlier, the decision to implement a coaching programme should never be conceived of as a simple 'add-on' or a 'quick win'. One way to ensure this does not happen is to explicitly link an implementation decision to the school's espoused values. It is not enough for there simply to be no obvious conflict between the school's stated *modus operandi*, and the fundamental nature and philosophy of coaching; it should be clear and obvious how a school's values are closely aligned with, and deliverable through coaching. Fundamentally a school's decision to embark on a coaching programme should be underpinned by the notion that 'this will help us to deliver what we are here to do'.

For example, at Halcyon London International School, where I spent a year as an interim headteacher, the stated values are 'innovation', 'collaboration' and 'community' (Halcyon London International School, 2022). It is clear to see that all three of these, along with associated values of problem-solving, wellbeing and inclusivity, are inherently deliverable through a coaching approach. Sure enough, coaching is fully embedded at Halcyon, with both teachers and students benefitting.

Growth Mindset thinking

Carol Dweck's work on Growth Mindset, which brought a cognitive scientific spin to the long-standing notion of the power of positive thinking, has had a significant impact in both educational and wider contexts. Unfortunately, as is often the case with popular ideas, it has also sometimes been the victim of simplistic interpretation and poor implementation.

Dweck's (2006) research suggested that Growth Mindset, the quality of believing that one can develop and improve in any area of endeavour, combined with a willingness to engage in struggle to do so, leads to associated changes in the brain and consequently higher levels of achievement. The elegant simplicity of Dweck's work has led many schools and businesses to embrace the idea. There are many examples of institutions seeking to develop a culture of Growth Mindset through motivational messaging, on posters, in assemblies or in meetings. Another common manifestation of this is a focus on praising the effort of students or employees, rather than their achievement. While there is nothing wrong, per se, with either of these things, Dweck herself has stated that seeking to foster Growth Mindset solely through such superficial means is unlikely to yield positive results: 'It is not about teaching the concept alone, it is much more about implementing practices that focus on growth and learning' (Dweck, 2020, p. 6).

Coaching practice, steeped as it is not only in fostering hope and positive thinking about personal and professional growth, but also in seeking and mapping pathways towards such growth, offers a platform for developing Growth Mindset in exactly the kind of practical manner that Dweck advocates.

But while we can see that coaching would seem to be an ideal vehicle for developing Growth Mindset thinking, it is also important to say that a coaching approach will not flourish in a school if it is not underpinned by an authentic commitment to Growth Mindset thinking. Chicken and egg.

Experience has shown me that some schools can confidently use the language of Growth Mindset, parroting statements such as 'mistakes are good because they are a source of learning and growth' and 'embrace challenge, without fear of failure', but not reflect this in the reality of their cultures. A school which penalises errors or limits opportunities for professional challenge, either directly through its structures and systems or indirectly through attitudes and the real nature of its professional relationships, does not offer the conditions for coaching to thrive in. For a coaching way to develop and survive in a school, Growth Mindset thinking has to be more than a set of visible artefacts in the hummock of its culture – it needs to be reflected in the actual nature of all the human interactions that take place there.

Engagement with scepticism

Most educators will be familiar with the 'Grumpy Sceptics', the group of teachers that seems to occupy a corner of every staff room on the planet, whose members have 'seen it all', know that 'this is just another fad' and feel that 'my way has always worked for me, why should I change?'

Coaching for professional development is as likely to be the subject of the Grumpy Sceptics' cynicism as any other initiative or project. Faced with such a response, it is tempting to characterise their scepticism as marginal, unhelpful and distracting, and to decide not to waste time and energy responding to it. In my view, this would not only be a mistake, but would also fly in the face of the philosophy and values associated with coaching. To this end, let's stop calling this group the Grumpy Sceptics and re-characterise them as 'Non-Conformist Questioners'. Such teachers are in reality likely to be experienced, often highly effective practitioners, who have indeed seen a number of educational trends come and go, and who are understandably wary of the possibility of resources (their own and the school's) being squandered on 'another initiative, which we won't be doing next year'. Ironically, the platform for critical professional reflection that coaching provides is exactly the sort of opportunity Non-Conformist Questioners may actually greatly appreciate. Moreover, coaching offers to this group the potential for individualised professional growth that they might not have found in other forms of CPD over the years.

For three important reasons, pro-active engagement with scepticism must be part of the culture which effectively underpins and supports a coaching approach to professional development:

1 Because failure to do so will often lead to resistance that may spread beyond the immediate group of Non-Conformist Questioners.
2 Because the experience and insight of sceptical teachers are often very useful in refining and improving the design and delivery of a programme.
3 Because to ignore or seek to marginalise those who question or who are sceptical about such a programme undermines important principles that frame a coaching mindset, for example active listening, seeking to understand and inclusivity.

The lower bummock

We now come to the most important and yet least 'visible' part of the coaching culture iceberg. The lower bummock provides the bedrock for all successful coaching programmes, yet there is only one element contained in this layer, and this element is encapsulated in just one small word; only one small word, but a word with hugely important implications: trust.

Trust

> Collective trust is a faculty's willingness to be vulnerable to another party based on the confidence that the latter party is benevolent, reliable, competent, honest, and open.
>
> (Forsyth et al., 2011, p. 35)

This simple yet compelling definition was created by academics from Ohio State University, and was distilled from many years of research in school settings; it perfectly encapsulates why trust is the single most important factor in successful school coaching programmes.

Essentially, when agreeing to be coached, a coachee is saying to themselves and their coach, 'I know there are elements of my teaching/leadership practice, which I need to develop in order to improve outcomes for students. I am willing to be open to the possibility of growth in areas I already know about and others that I am yet to identify. This may be challenging at times but I believe that you have my best interest at heart. I trust you. Let's go there.'

This openness to vulnerability is unlikely to occur if there is any suspicion at all of a hidden agenda or if past behaviour/events have indicated that there is professional risk involved in such openness.

Let's take, in turn, each characteristic described by Forsyth as leading to collective trust, and reflect on what they might mean when we apply them specifically to the context of developing a coaching culture.

Benevolence and honesty

Honesty and a desire to do good for other people may seem obvious qualities for any person working in education to have. However, dishonesty, self-interest and political manoeuvring can manifest in schools, just as they do in other fields of human activity. Unfortunately, there is evidence that cultures of pole-climbing and back-covering are becoming more prevalent in schools, especially those which tend to look to the corporate sector for their style and approach. I am not saying that schools have nothing to learn from the business world, but when personal advancement and sometimes ruthless competition become key features of a school culture, it is difficult to embed a coaching approach in a truly meaningful way. In an authentic coaching culture, mistakes are a source of learning and growth, not political currency to be banked by others for their own agendas. In an authentic coaching culture, the truth is embraced, even when it is uncomfortable to do so. In an authentic coaching culture, a concern for colleagues is not part of a quid pro quo calculation, rather, it is a manifestation of a fundamental belief in the importance of education for the good of all.

Reliability and competence

Trust is as dependent on the competence of others, as it is on confidence in others. It is also heavily reliant on factors as prosaic as the ability of another party to organise themselves to do what they say they are going to do. If authentic benevolence expressed through coaching conversations is not backed up by an ability to follow through on whatever is discussed and to realise any actions that are agreed, a coachee is likely to quickly, and understandably, lose faith in the process. Similarly, the establishment of genuine professional trust is also dependent on a belief in the credibility of other parties (Aristotle would say, their 'ethos'). In this case, we mean credibility related to professional knowledge. A culture of professional inquiry and a commitment to knowledge building are important companions to a coaching approach. Coaching conversations cannot afford to draw on outdated, inaccurate or misleading notions of what works in the classroom or in school leadership. In this case, collective trust is facilitated by a belief that all parties are showing each other professional respect by committing to remaining well informed and to sharing reliable knowledge for the benefit of each other, and of the students in the school.

Openness

This is perhaps the most important, yet most difficult to develop characteristic of collective trust. In my view, openness, in this sense, goes beyond notions of honesty, transparency and authenticity. Here, I think we are talking about pro-active openness, a willingness to seek out and wrestle with difficult notions, not just 'elephants in the room' but also 'mice beneath the floorboards'. Groups of professionals who are willing to challenge themselves and each other to question assumptions, who resist groupthink and who refuse to settle for simple solutions and embrace complexity, are, in my view, manifesting trust in its purest form.

Understanding and managing change

It is likely that any sort of move towards developing a coaching approach to CPD in a school will involve a degree of change. Much has been written about change management over the years, but when thinking about this, in specific relation to implementing and sustaining a coaching approach in a school, I believe the work of Michael Fullan is both highly pertinent and very useful.

Fullan's (2020) seminal book, *Leading in a Culture of Change*, was written primarily with a school audience in mind but its influence has been felt beyond the education sector. Fullan claimed that there is 'a remarkable convergence of theories, knowledge bases and strategies that … create a new mindset for thinking about and leading complex change' (ibid., p. 8). From this convergence, Fullan distilled his model of leadership of change, which consists of five components:

1 moral purpose;
2 nuance (understanding change);
3 relationships, relationships, relationships;
4 knowledge building and deep learning;
5 coherence making.

(ibid., p. 9)

All of these are framed by the leadership 'attitudes' of enthusiasm, hope and energy.

In Figure 6.2, I have applied Fullan's framework to illustrate the type of key messaging associated with each component of change management that leaders may use when introducing a coaching approach to CPD in their schools.

Fullan's model implies that pro-active communication is crucial to the successful management of change initiatives, and specifically, the clarity and consistency of this communication. It is also important that communication strategies take into account the fact that change tends to evoke differing responses at different times during the process. Research suggests that teachers pass through particular 'stages of concern' when a change initiative is implemented (Hall and Hord, 2011):

Figure 6.2 Leading change – introducing a coaching approach to CPD

0 A lack of awareness of/concern about the change.

1 A growing awareness of the change and a desire for information.

2 Questions about how the change will affect day-to-day work.

3 Concerns about the time that will be needed to implement the new approach.

4 Focus on impact on students.

5 A growing willingness to work with others to make the initiative work.

6 A sense of 'ownership' of the change and willingness to adapt and refine the initiative to increase its impact.

Awareness of these stages and their emotional impact will help leaders craft their communication to address these concerns directly and to support teachers in moving towards an acceptance and embracing of change.

At this stage it is useful to issue a word of warning about the 'implementation dip'. Defined as a drop 'in performance and confidence as one encounters an innovation that requires new skills and understandings' (Fullan, 2001, p. 40), the implementation dip is a usually temporary, but possibly fatal phenomenon. While a pro-active and empathetic approach to leading and communicating about new initiatives may head off some of its effects, the

Figure 6.3 The implementation dip – introducing a coaching approach to CPD

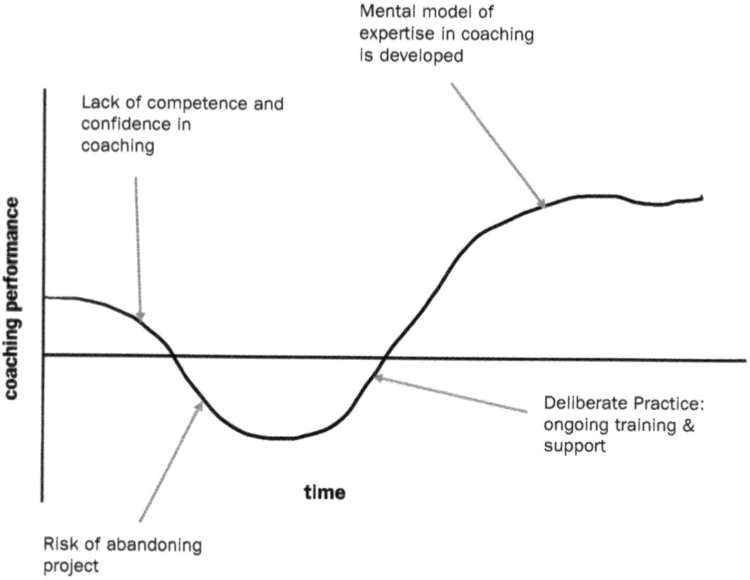

social-psychological impact of change, as well as the challenge of developing new skills and approaches, often do lead to an early dip in performance in the area being developed. This is in line with what we know about the introduction of new skills in the classroom and resonates with the idea of 'productive struggle'. When new content is initially introduced, students will often encounter a degree of success in understanding and using this, due to the scaffolded support that tends to be provided at this stage. However, once they move on to independent practice, students will often struggle to reproduce their earlier successes and, unless encouraged and supported to understand that this is a necessary part of the learning process, this can lead to them losing heart and giving up.

Let's apply the concept of the implementation dip to a school professional development context, specifically the introduction of a new coaching programme. We can assume that a rigorous, well-designed and engaging training programme is likely to lead to a degree of early confidence and a sense of competence in teachers involved in a coaching initiative. However, once this period is over and staff are moving on to implementing coaching in their day-to-day work, there is a strong possibility that challenges encountered and a lack of proficiency will lead to a drop in confidence and performance, an implementation dip.

At this stage, as teachers potentially become disillusioned and disengaged, there is a real risk that the project will be abandoned. Communication becomes even more crucial at this stage, with leaders needing to acknowledge the challenges, offer appropriate support, and crucially point out that this stage of productive struggle is a necessary part of a process which will ultimately lead to a successfully embedded programme.

An example of what an implementation dip in the context of the introduction of a school coaching programme might look like, is illustrated in Figure 6.3.

Summary

We have seen that organisational culture is a notoriously slippery concept. We have also seen that if a school is to introduce a coaching approach, the culture of the institution needs to both reflect and be defined by the values and principles of coaching. Put another way, we don't know precisely what culture is, but if it's not right, then a coaching approach is unlikely to take root and thrive.

Leaders considering introducing coaching need to look honestly at the culture that exists in their schools and ask themselves fundamental questions about their institution's priorities and values and whether they coincide with a coaching approach. A school that is primarily motivated to introduce coaching for reasons such as it seeming to be in line with current perceptions of 'good practice' or because it is 'what all the other schools seem to be doing', is in danger of massively missing the point. Coaching cannot be seen as an add-on to a school's way of doing things; in schools where it is successful, coaching *is* the way of doing things.

7 Howick College

Placing coaching at the heart of professional learning

There are many schools around the world which have successfully embraced coaching as an approach to professional development. These schools vary in terms of their type, size and context, as well as the purpose and nature of the coaching programme they have developed. This chapter seeks to bring together some of the themes developed earlier in the book through a case study of one such school, Howick College in Auckland, New Zealand. The purpose of this is not to provide a rigid 'template' for other schools to model their own approach on; rather, to allow the reader to gain insight into what the reality of a coaching culture looks like in one particular school, and the journey involved in developing this, so that they can apply any relevant learnings to their own particular context.

Howick College is a co-educational, government-funded school in an eastern suburb of Auckland, New Zealand. The school serves a diverse population of over 2000 students aged between 12 and 18, and seeks to ensure that its 4C values (Courtesy, Commitment, Curiosity and Courage) permeate all aspects of school life for staff and students. This case study of Howick College's coaching programme is based on an interview with the school's Associate Principal and coaching lead, Dr Paul Bennett, which was carried out in November 2021.

Development of the programme

Coaching for professional development at Howick College was born out of three key factors:

1   a school board and leadership team which were looking for a professional learning programme that was both individualised and had the potential to deliver strategic goals;

2 the appointment of a senior leader with extensive knowledge and experience of coaching in school settings;

3 the allocation of funding and time to the development and roll-out of the programme.

Clearly, the elements of strong leadership and allocation of resource, alluded to in Chapter 6 as crucial to the success of coaching initiatives, were present from the beginning of the coaching project at Howick. This provided a strong underpinning to its development from that point onwards.

On joining the school as an Associate Principal, Paul Bennett brought with him both an in-depth academic knowledge and practical experience of coaching in schools, and he was therefore able to apply this in helping the school develop its plans to deliver a vision of professional learning through a coaching approach across the college.

The delivery of this vision was further supported by the success of an application for funding through the New Zealand government's 'Investing in Educational Success' initiative. In order to obtain this funding, Howick joined together with a number of schools to form a Community of Learning or Kāhui Ako, which proposed placing coaching at the heart of a collaborative project to improve teacher capability and therefore outcomes for students. The funding enabled Howick to create 12 teacher coaches, each of whom was able to allocate four hours of their working week to their role. Crucially the funding also allowed for an extensive training programme to be rolled out before coaches started working with teachers. This programme extended over a period of six months and through opportunities for external input, experimentation, reflection, collaboration and incremental improvement, coaches had reached a level of expertise before they started working with colleagues. This thorough and rigorous programme of preparation is identified by Paul Bennett as a crucial factor in the success of the Howick project. His own experience and research had shown him that many similar initiatives fail because coaches are not given enough time to learn and practise the skills, and that the result of this was often that teachers had poor experiences, leading to programme failure.

Bennett identifies that a level of preparatory training is also required for all teachers before they experience being coached, recognising that this was something that was not fully considered when the Howick programme was initially rolled out. The result of this was that as 12 well-trained, enthusiastic 'coaching gurus' set about their work, the teachers being coached didn't at first fully appreciate what coaching was, nor why it was being implemented, meaning that there were a few bumps in the road as the programme launched.

Responding to this, Howick now provides an introduction to inquiry and the school's coaching approach as part of its new staff induction programme. This covers the basics of coaching and how it links to the school's approach to teacher development, as well as New Zealand's mandated professional learning requirements.

Nature of the programme

The numbers associated with Howick College's coaching programme are impressive and reflect the school's commitment to the approach. Each member of the faculty (over 130 teachers) receives a coaching session every fortnight. To deliver this, each of the 12 coaches is allocated between eight and ten coachees. Timetabling largely defines which coaches work with which coachees, with the matching process being governed by the coincidence of non-teaching periods of both coaches and coachees. This means that coach and coachee may not teach the same subject or work with the same students, a feature which Bennett identifies as a strength, given the fact that the coach will often have a resulting 'neutrality', which enables a facilitative rather than a directive approach to be taken.

In addition to time spent working with colleagues, coaches also meet together as a group with the coaching lead and members of SLT once a week. These sessions are largely used for 'supervision', a process which many qualified coaches engage with, and which essentially consists of reflecting on and discussing coaching practice for the purpose of development and improvement. The sessions also involve ongoing training and collaborative work to ensure the programme is running smoothly. These meetings are a good example of the importance of ongoing training and development being built into coaching programmes, even those which are well embedded.

Howick's emphasis on ongoing training is complemented by a strong focus on feedback for improvement. All coachees are asked twice a year to complete a questionnaire on their experience of being coached. The coaching lead meets individually with all coaches to reflect on feedback received, to identify strengths, weaknesses and trends and to make plans for development. Similarly, coaches will regularly record videos of their sessions, and then, guided by a specially designed rubric, analyse and critique their practice with colleagues.

Coaching at Howick is framed by 'Spirals of Inquiry', a system for developing professional agency widely used in New Zealand. The process is used to identify and work with 'problems of practice' through six stages:

1 Scanning: What's happening for learners in my class?

2 Focusing: Which is the area that will make the biggest difference for learners if we focus on this?

3 Developing a hunch: How is my practice contributing to this area?

4 New learning: What do I need to learn to improve my practice in this area?

5 Taking action: What are the things I can try to make a difference in this area?

6 Checking: How do I know if it's working?

(Timperley et al., 2022)

Bennett stresses that central to the success of this approach is the existence of professional trust; this relates not only to the relationship between coach and coachee, but also to the trust that the teacher has in the coaching system and the school's reasons for implementing it. We saw in Chapter 6 that authentic professional trust is the absolute bedrock of any successful coaching programme, and Bennett emphasises that, while year 1 of the programme rollout at Howick was very much about establishing systems and routines, year 2 was focused on building and sustaining relationships of professional trust; – hard work, but essential for the viability of the project.

When asked how Howick set about making clear the separation between appraisal and coaching at the school, Bennett first points out that this is actually no longer an issue, because, as of 2021, the New Zealand Ministry of Education is in the process of phasing out teacher performance appraisal, and replacing this with Professional Growth Cycles, which are driven by development, rather than accountability. However, he goes on to say that before this initiative, the school took great care to make very clear to all teachers the difference between the two systems, with appraisal being explained as something done once a year with a Department Head to ensure professional standards are being met, while coaching was a time for risk-taking, experimentation, and as he puts it, 'playing in the sandpit'. Bennett goes on to say that, in fact, when the two systems were explained in induction meetings, this message was further emphasised by the fact that the PowerPoint slides outlining the coaching process were in full colour, while the slides which explained the appraisal system were presented in a more mundane black and white (design features which apparently happened by accident, but which were retained)!

Measuring the impact of the programme

Another important feature of coaching at Howick is the emphasis placed on tracking outcomes and evaluating impact. Early in the project, the school took a decision not to build their programme around whole school development priorities, rather seeking to ensure that areas of focus for each teacher's coaching were based on their own professional needs. This meant that a 'one-size-fits-all' system for measuring impact would not work for the school, and they had to seek a way of evaluating impact that reflected the wide range of foci the system would produce.

In order to do this, Howick's outcome measuring system is framed by a focus on triangulation, the gathering of multiple forms of evidence of impact, which are cross-referenced. Thus, once a problem of practice has been identified by the coach and coachee and plans developed for moving forward, they will agree two to three ways in which they will evaluate the impact of the coaching on the identified area. For example, a plan to reduce the number of students from a particular group, who have been moving around the classroom inappropriately, may include an agreement to collect the following forms of evidence of impact: videos taken at different times to compare the levels of inappropriate movement; student interviews and feedback; and anecdotal teacher reporting. On the other hand, tracking the impact of coaching on problems of practice related more directly to student learning may involve the gathering and comparison of attainment data of differing types.

Whichever impact assessment methods are agreed, the details and results of these are entered onto a single database, thereby creating a rich source of information about the programme and allowing the school to appraise its overall impact, as well as to identify any patterns and trends in the problems of practice being identified and the approaches being used to tackle them. This is useful, not only to the board and senior leadership in identifying common challenges, which may feed into decisions about whole school strategic improvement initiatives, but also in terms of the possibility of creating collaborative communities of inquiry, consisting of teachers with similar problems of practice who, by working together, can compare and contrast the effectiveness of their differing approaches to solving these.

Future of the programme

Bennett stresses that it was only after two years of training, tweaking and trust-building, that the school started to really see the full benefits of its coaching programme. This highlights the importance of understanding and pushing through the implementation dip (see p. 88) and also the fact that the introduction of coaching into a school needs to be regarded as a long-term project, as it involves not only changes in systems but also new ways of thinking about teaching and how we improve as professionals.

The importance of succession planning is something Howick has learned about as its programme has developed, and which is now factored into thinking about the future. Obviously, teachers come and go from schools and this is something Howick now takes into account in its planning for ongoing training, not only of new coaches but also potentially for those in strategic leadership roles who play a vital role in sustaining the project.

At the time of writing, Howick is ready to push on with its coaching programme, having moved, as Bennett describes it, from a place where teachers are coached because the people in charge are telling them they have to be, to a place where teachers and leaders actively seek out coaching, formal or otherwise, for any problems or issues they are facing.

Bennett identifies two major areas of focus for the programme's future development:

1 The introduction of coaching for students, initially as part of the current student leadership programme but eventually extending more widely, with the possibility of teachers coaching students as part of their pastoral role, and also exploring the idea of students coaching students.
2 Team coaching at a departmental level, with middle leaders being trained in group coaching and using this to facilitate collaborative working with problems of practice which exist across a subject area.

Take-aways

The ongoing success of Howick College's coaching programme is testament to Paul Bennett's leadership of the programme, alongside Deputy Principal, Tina Filipo, as well as to the commitment to the approach demonstrated by the school's board and wider leadership team. Certainly, this is a good illustration of the fundamental importance of strong and effective leadership for any school coaching programme. The complexity of the coaching landscape is such that expertise and in-depth knowledge are vital to help guide teams through misconceptions, avoid poor practice and, crucially, head off lethal mutations.

In addition to the importance of leadership, this case study also serves to illustrate the role in the creation of a successful programme, of the different levels of the 'coaching culture iceberg' explored in Chapter 6.

Hummock (the most immediately visible elements of a coaching culture)

1 *Dedicated resource*: Paul Bennett is very clear that the success of the coaching programme at Howick is, to a great degree, attributable to the school's willingness and ability to make financial and temporal resources available for it. In this case, a grant was successfully applied for, which allowed coaches to be released from some of their teaching hours in order to be trained and to carry out their coaching duties. Clearly, not every school has access to such additional funding, but if a school is serious about reaping the benefits of the approach, it will need to allocate sufficient money and time to the project either by finding savings elsewhere or through efficiencies; coaching cannot be done on the cheap.

2 *Implementation planning*: Again, Bennett stresses the vital importance of planned, plentiful and ongoing training in Howick's coaching programme. Such training is provided for coaches, teachers and leaders alike and provides the backbone of sustainable implementation over time.

3 *Shared language*: Ensuring that all stakeholders both understand and consistently apply the language of coaching has been crucial in maintaining fidelity to the project's aims and intentions. This is linked to the ongoing training referred to above.

Upper bummock (just below the waterline, not immediately visible)

1 *Links with school values:* Howick College's stated values, as outlined below, appear to dovetail perfectly with the values typically associated with coaching and the professional relationships the approach fosters.

Courtesy – We will be kind and respectful

Commitment – We will never give up

Curiosity – We will strive to understand

Courage – We will challenge ourselves

(Howick College, 2022)

2 *Growth Mindset thinking*: Growth Mindset thinking is characterised by a willingness to make and learn from mistakes. For this to exist in an organisation, it must be underpinned by 'psychological safety', a universally held knowledge in the institution that making mistakes will not be held against you. Amy Edmondson, the psychologist who introduced the concept of psychological safety, suggests that there are three things that people can do to foster team psychological safety: 'Frame the work as a learning problem, not an execution problem. Acknowledge your own fallibility. Model curiosity and ask lots of questions' (Edmondson, 2019, p. 154). While it is beyond the scope of this case study to ascertain the extent to which stakeholders at Howick model the second of Edmondson's suggested actions, 'acknowledge your own fallibility', we can see that the other two of these actions are very much reflected in Howick's approach to coaching. The school's use of the idea of 'problems of practice' to frame coaching conversations resonates with Edmondson's notion of learning problems: that when assessing the outcome of a project, one should not look just at the 'results', rather that useful learning that comes from the process should also be factored into notions of 'success'. Similarly, the instruction to 'model curiosity and ask lots of questions' can be seen as fundamental to all good coaching practice, and almost exactly mirrored in the Spiral of Inquiry authors' stated central argument that 'innovation floats on a sea of inquiry and curiosity is a driver for change' (Timperley et al., 2014, p. 4).

3 *Engagement with cynicism*: As described above, Howick did receive push-back from some teachers as their coaching programme got under way. In retrospect, the school could see that this was largely down to a lack of training for teachers, which meant they did not have a full understanding of coaching, the programme or how it would benefit them. In the light of this, rather than 'pushing on regardless', the project leaders ensured the coaches were ready to respond to questions and doubts and to 'go gently' in their sessions, so that teachers were less likely to feel overwhelmed or threatened by the process.

Lower bummock (the least tangible, yet most important factor): trust

As we have already seen, establishing and building trust in the system of coaching, and in the relationships that underpin the system, were an explicit focus in the development of the programme at Howick. Although it is beyond the scope of this case study to gauge the degree to which teachers at the school trust in the process, to an extent, the proof is in the pudding. The fact that the coaching system at Howick College continues to develop and thrive is strong evidence that stakeholders at the school have faith and trust in the programme; without this, there is every chance the programme would have withered and died.

Conclusion

I conclude this book with two personal stories. As well as highlighting some of the themes explored so far, these also serve to illustrate the fact that my belief in the power of coaching and the impact it has on education professionals is informed by more than research alone. Rather than stories about coaching, these are stories about an absence of coaching. Occurring at different times in my school career, I now look back at what happened, and see that both situations might well have turned out differently, had I had access to some sort of coaching support at those times. The first story is about the misplaced confidence of a young teacher. The second story is about the mental health crisis of a school leader.

Going into my third year of teaching in a small London primary school, I was doing pretty well, or at least I thought so. The kids seemed to like me. The feedback from my observations was consistently good. I was on top of the curriculum content. However, at the beginning of that year, a new headteacher joined us and everything changed. As part of 'getting to know the school', she spent a lot of time visiting classes and talking to teachers about what she observed. When she spoke with me about my classroom, a theme began to emerge: it was quite a noisy environment, too many children were off-task, I wasn't consistent in my behaviour management. This feedback wasn't what I was used to hearing and certainly wasn't in line with the story I told myself about my teaching, which was that it facilitated active, engaged learning in my students. So, my initial reaction was to pretty much ignore the feedback. Up to now I had been told that my teaching was fine – who was this new person to say there were areas I needed to improve in? I skipped through the behaviour management book she lent me, I may even have tried out a couple of the techniques in it, but nothing significant changed in the way I was teaching. Then she made the suggestion that I should observe two of my colleagues teaching, in order to see how they managed behaviour in their classrooms. In both cases, I was equally awestruck and disheartened by the experience. Here were two teachers, very different in their style and approach, but both seemingly able, without any noticeable effort, to create a magical atmosphere, where happy, focused children interacted calmly with each other and their teacher. These classrooms were nothing like mine and immediately

I could see what my headteacher was getting at. As I watched these geniuses at work, I frantically tried to take notes so that I could try out some of their magic in my own classroom. The problem was, I didn't know what to write down. There didn't seem to be any particular secret to their success, they just seemed to 'do it', and what's more, they both 'did it' in very different ways. Both teachers were very kind, and gave me a few tips after I had observed them, but when I took these back into my classroom, they just didn't have the same effect and I quickly abandoned them. Very rapidly, I had moved from being a content coaster, sure of my ability in the classroom, to being a struggling survivor, confused about how to improve my teaching and trying to get by, one day at a time. It took me some time to regain my confidence.

Thirty years on, I can see how a coach might have been able to help that struggling teacher.

First, a coach is likely to have prevented me from becoming a content coaster in the first place. Through supportive challenge, I would have been invited to reflect on my practice and supported to identify areas for improvement, and strategies to deliver that improvement.

Second, a coach would have helped me to avoid feeling overwhelmed by the nature of my challenge and the sheer number of possible strategies and approaches that I was presented with when reading the book, observing my colleagues and receiving their tips. A coach would have helped me choose one or two strategies to work with and to manage my cognitive load by focusing on those.

Lastly, a coach would have been an ongoing presence in my development and would have helped me overcome the sense of professional isolation that I experienced during that year.

And so, on to the second story. This finds me a year into a new senior leadership role and battling with the size and complexity of the challenges I am faced with. Some of the things on my plate were: challenging parents, school owners with values that conflicted with my own, highly complex curriculum issues, falling rolls, and a dysfunctional shared building arrangement, among many others. I lived some distance from the school and had to drive at least an hour each way through terrible traffic – I would leave home at 6 am and get home at 8 pm, and then not sleep much because my head was spinning. I knew I was struggling but I was The Principal, so 'I had to be strong'. I kept going and kept going, until the inevitable happened. I crashed. I was signed off for six weeks with clinical depression and anxiety.

It is important to stress straight away that coaching was not used in this case, and indeed never should be used, as a response to mental health issues; to help me in this area, I worked with a therapist who helped me to recover and move forward positively. However, I do believe a good coach might well have helped me to avoid crashing in the first instance. Effective coaching allows a coachee to gain perspective, to reflect and realise new insights, to make plans and to move forward. I lacked the headspace to do any of this on my own and I stubbornly refused to seek out help. Structured and systematic access to coaching would have taken this out of my hands.

The professional roles of teacher and school leader are complex, demanding and challenging in nature. Introducing a coaching approach in schools will not change this. However, when delivered with careful planning, integrity and sufficient resources, I do believe coaching has the potential to make schools places where optimism and a genuine and realisable commitment to meaningful development across the whole staff can thrive.

References

Albornoz, F. et al. (2017) Training to teach science: Experimental evidence from Argentina. [Online] Available at: https://www.nottingham.ac.uk/credit/documents/papers/2017/17-08.pdf (accessed 31 December 2021).

Allen, J., Yee Mikami, A., Gregory, A. and Lun, J. (2011) An interaction-based approach to enhancing secondary school instruction and student achievement. *Science*, 333(6045): 1034–7.

Allen, R. (2019) If CPD is so important, then why is so much of it so bad? [Online] Available at: https://rebeccaallen.co.uk/2019/01/16/if-cpd-is-so-important-then-why-is-so-much-of-it-so-bad/ (accessed 25 November 2021).

Ambition Institute (2017) Incremental coaching. [Online] Available at: https://s3.eu-west-2.amazonaws.com/ambition-institute/documents/Incremental_Coaching_-_12-page_report_summary.pdf (accessed 22 December 2021).

Anderson, M. and Shannon, A. (1988) Toward a conceptualization of mentoring. *Journal of Teacher Education*, 39(1): 38–42.

Australian Academy of Science (2018) How practice changes the brain. [Online] Available at: https://www.science.org.au/curious/people-medicine/how-practice-changes-brain (accessed 26 January 2022).

Bambrick-Santoyo, P. (2018) *Leverage Leadership 2.0*. San Francisco: Jossey-Bass.

Barker, J. and Rees, T. (2020) Expertise, mental models and leadership knowledge. [Online] Available at: https://www.ambition.org.uk/blog/expertise-mental-models-and-leadership-knowledge/ (accessed 28 January 2022).

Bill and Melinda Gates Foundation (2013) Measures of effective teaching project releases final research report. [Online] Available at: https://www.gatesfoundation.org/ideas/media-center/press-releases/2013/01/measures-of-effective-teaching-project-releases-final-research-report (accessed 9 February 2022).

Bjork, R. (1994) Memory and meta-memory considerations in the training of human beings. In J. S. A. Metcalfe (ed.) *Metacognition: Knowing about Knowing*. Cambridge, MA: MIT Press, pp. 185–205.

Bosman, M. (2021) Neurocoaching: A brain-minded approach to facilitate transformation. [Online] Available at: https://stratleader.net/sli-blog/neurocoaching (accessed 4 February 2022).

Buck, A. (2020) *The BASIC Coaching Method*. London: Cadogan Press.

Burns, D. (1981) *Feeling Good: The New Mood Therapy*. New York: Penguin Books.

Cherry, K. (2020) 5 things you can do to achieve flow. [Online] Available at: https://www.verywellmind.com/ways-to-achieve-flow-2794769 (accessed 16 January 2022).

Coe, R. (2013) *Improving Education: A Triumph of Hope over Experience.* Durham: Centre for Evaluation and Monitoring.

Collins, K. (2017) The importance of randomised controlled trials in education. *Impact*, May, pp. 12–13.

Cordingley, P. et al. (2015) *Developing Great Teaching: Lessons from the International Reviews into Effective Professional Development,* London: Teacher Development Trust.

Covey, S. (1989) *The 7 Habits of Highly Effective People.* New York: Simon & Schuster.

Csikszentmihalyi, M. (1990) *Flow: The Psychology of Optimal Experience.* New York: Harper and Row.

Deans for Impact (2016) Practice with purpose. [Online] Available at: https://deansforimpact.org/wp-content/uploads/2016/12/Practice-with-Purpose_FOR-PRINT_113016.pdf (accessed 26 January 2022).

Department for Education (2016) Standard for teachers' professional development. [Online] Available at: https://assets.publishing.service.gov.uk/government/uploads/system/uploads/attachment_data/file/537030/160712_-_PD_standard.pdf (accessed 25 November 2021).

Department for Education (2020) Headteachers' standards 2020. [Online] Available at: https://www.gov.uk/government/publications/national-standards-of-excellence-for-headteachers/headteachers-standards-2020 (accessed 17 December 2021).

Dweck, C. (2006) *Mindset: How You Can Fulfil Your Potential.* New York: Random House.

Dweck, C. (2020) Growth Mindset: Where did it go wrong? *TES*, 11 April, p. 6.

Ebbinghaus, H. (1885) *Memory: A Contribution to Experimental Psychology.* New York: Teacher's College, Columbia University.

Edmondson, A. (2019) *The Fearless Organization.* Hoboken, NJ: John Wiley & Sons.

Education Endowment Foundation (2019) Putting evidence to work: A school's guide to implementation. [Online] Available at: https://d2tic4wvo1iusb.cloudfront.net/eef-guidance-reports/implementation/EEF_Implementation_Guidance_Report_2019.pdf?v=1635355218 (accessed 10 February 2022).

Education Endowment Foundation (2021) *Effective Professional Development.* London: EEF.

Education Policy Institute (2021a) The pandemic and teacher attrition: An exodus waiting to happen? [Online] Available at: https://epi.org.uk/publications-and-research/the-pandemic-and-teacher-attrition-an-exodus-waiting-to-happen/ (accessed 12 July 2022).

Education Policy Institute (2021b) The effects of high-quality professional development on teachers and students. [Online] Available at: https://epi.org.uk/publications-and-research/effects (accessed 12 July 2022).

Education Support (2021) Teacher Wellbeing Index 2021. [Online] Available at: https://www.educationsupport.org.uk/media/5pgbh1bn/twix_2021_3_mental_health_of_education_staff.pdf (accessed 17 December 2021).

Einhorn, C. (2018) The AREA Method: Warren Buffett and untangling your plate of spaghetti. [Online] Available at: https://www.areamethod.com/the-area-method-warren-buffett-untangling-your-plate-of-spaghetti/ (accessed 17 December 2021).

Ericsson, A., Krampe, R. and Tesch-Romer, C. (1993) The role of deliberate practice in the acquisition of expert performance. *Psychological Review*, 100(3): 363–406.

Forsyth, P., Adams, C. and Hoy, W. (2011) *Collective Trust: Why Schools Can't Improve Without It*. New York: Teachers College Press.

Fullan, M. (2001) *Leading in a Culture of Change*. San Francisco: Jossey-Bass.

Fullan, M. (2020) *Leading in a Culture of Change*. 2nd edn. San Francisco: Jossey-Bass.

Gallwey, T. (1974) *The Inner Game of Tennis*. New York: Random House.

Geary, J. (2009) Ted talks: Metaphorically speaking. [Online] Available at: https://www.ted.com/talks/james_geary_metaphorically_speaking?language=en#t-15054 (accessed 6 December 2021).

Gladwell, M. (2008) *The Outliers*. New York: Little, Brown and Company.

Goleman, D. (1995) *Emotional Intelligence*. New York: Bantam Books.

Grenville-Giddings, B. (2021) Good professional development for teaching SEND is good professional development for all. [Online] Available at: https://researchschool.org.uk/derby/news/good-professional-development-for-teaching-send-is-good-professional-development-for-all-the-importance-of-creating-a-shared-language (accessed 3 March 2022).

Grossman, P. et al. (2009) Teaching practice: A cross-professional perspective. *Teachers College Record*, 111(9): 2055–100.

Halcyon London International School (2022) Mission: Who we are. [Online] Available at: https://halcyonschool.com/who-we-are/ (accessed 8 March 2022).

Hall, G. and Hord, S. (2011) *Implementing Change: Patterns, Principles, and Potholes*. 3rd edn. Upper Saddle River, NJ: Pearson.

Hattie, J. (2018) Collective Teacher Efficacy (CTE) according to John Hattie. [Online] Available at: https://visible-learning.org/2018/03/collective-teacher-efficacy-hattie/ (accessed 29 December 2021).

Hattie, J. (2019) Hattie Ranking: 252 influences and effect sizes related to student achievement. [Online] Available at: https://visible-learning.org/hattie-ranking-influences-effect-sizes-learning-achievement/ (accessed 29 December 2021).

Hobbis, M., Sims, S. and Allen, R. (2021) Habit formation limits growth in teacher effectiveness: A review of converging evidence from neuroscience and social science. *Review of Education*, 9(1): 3–23.

Hollweck, T. and Lofthouse, R. (2021) Contextual coaching: Levering and leading school improvement through collaborative professionalism. *International Journal of Mentoring and Coaching in Education*, 10(4): 399–417.

Hoogsteen, T. (2020) Collective efficacy: Toward a new narrative of its development and role in achievement. *Palgrave Communications*, 6(2). https://doi.org/10.1057/s41599-019-0381-z.

Howick College (2022) Vision and values. [Online] Available at: https://www.howickcollege.school.nz/vision-values (accessed 12 April 2022).

IBIS World (2021) Business coaching in the US. [Online] Available at: https://www.ibisworld.com/industry-statistics/market-size/business-coaching-united-states/ (accessed 9 December 2021).

Jerrim, J., Sims, S., Taylor, H. and Allen, R. (2021) Has the mental health and wellbeing of teachers in England changed over time? New evidence from three datasets. *Oxford Review of Education*, 47(6): 805–25.

Kahneman, D. (2011) *Thinking, Fast and Slow*. London: Penguin.

Kalyuga, S., Ayres, P., Chandler, P. and Sweller, J. (2011) The expertise reversal effect. *Educational Psychologist*, 38(1): 23–31.

Kaufman, T. (2021) The brain science of building positive relationships with students. [Online] Available at: https://www.understood.org/articles/es-mx/brain-science-says-4-reasons-to-build-positive-relationships-with-students (accessed 3 February 2022).

Kidger, J. et al. (2016) Teachers' wellbeing and depressive symptoms, and associated risk factors: A large cross-sectional study in English secondary schools. *Journal of Affective Disorders*, 192(1): 76–82.

Kirschner, P., Sweller, J. and Clark, R. (2006) Why minimal guidance during instruction does not work: An analysis of the failure of constructivist, discovery, problem-based, experiential, and inquiry-based teaching. *Educational Psychologist*, 41(2): 75–86.

Knight, J. (1999) Partnership learning: Putting conversation at the heart of professional development. [Online] Available at: https://www.instructionalcoaching.com/Research/Partnership-Learning/Partnership-Learning-AERA1999.pdf (accessed 22 December 2021).

Knight, J. (2018) *The Impact Cycle*. London: Corwin.

Knoster, T., Villa, R. and Thousand, J. (2000) 'A framework for thinking about systems change', in Villa, R. and Thousand, J. (eds) *Restructuring for Caring and Effective Education: Piecing the Puzzle Together*, pp. 93–128. Baltimore, Paul H. Brookes Publishing.

Kraft, M., Blazar, D. and Hogan, D. (2018) The effect of teacher coaching on instruction and achievement: A meta-analysis of the causal evidence. *Review of Educational Research*, 88(4): 547–88.

Lilley, G. (2016) Effect size. [Online] Available at: http://visablelearning.blogspot.com/p/effect-size.html (accessed 29 December 2021).

Lofthouse, R. and Whiteside, R. (2020) *Sustaining a Vital Profession*. Leeds: Leeds Beckett University.

Lovell, O. (n.d.) Effect sizes, robust or bogus? Reflections from my discussions with Hattie and Simpson. [Online] Available at: https://www.ollielovell.com/on-education/effect-sizes/ (accessed 30 December 2021).

McGovern, J. (2001) Maximising the impact of executive coaching. *The Manchester Review*, 6(1): 3–11.

McGowan, S. and Behar, E. (2013) A preliminary investigation of stimulus control training for worry: Effects on anxiety and insomnia. *Behavior Modification*, 37(1): 90–112.

Moore, C. (2019) Learned optimism: Is Martin Seligman's glass half full? [Online] Available at: https://positivepsychology.com/learned-optimism/ (accessed 13 January 2022).

National Centre for Social Research for CUBeC (2012) *What Influences Teachers to Change their Practice? A Rapid Research Review*. Bristol: author.

OECD (2018) *Teachers and School Leaders as Lifelong Learners*. Paris: OECD Publishing.

OECD (2019) *Teachers and School Leaders as Lifelong Learners.* Paris: OECD Publishing.

O'Mahony, G. (2004) *Innovation in Headteacher Induction, Case Study 2: SAGE Principal Mentor Program.* London: National College for School Leadership.

Paul, R. and Elder, L. (2016) *The Thinker's Guide to the Art of Socratic Questioning.* London: Rowman & Littlefield.

Psychology Today (2021) Intuition. [Online] Available at: https://www.psychologytoday.com/gb/basics/intuition (accessed 30 November 2021).

Raybould, R., Hamilton, P. and Rigby, H. (2021) Heads coaching heads for school improvement. *Impact,* September, pp. 22–4.

Rumelt, R. (2012) *Good Strategy, Bad Strategy.* 2nd edn. London: Profile Books.

Schein, E. (1985) *Organizational Culture and Leadership: A Dynamic View.* San Francisco: Jossey-Bass.

School Dash (2020) Personnel development. [Online] Available at: https://www.schooldash.com/blog-2011.html#20201118 (accessed 24 November 2021).

Scomis (2017) The Teacher Workload Report. Available at: https://www.groupcall.com/hubfs/Scomis%20-%20The%20teacher%20workload%20report.pdf (accessed 14 July 2022).

Seligman, M. (2013) *Flourish: A Visionary New Understanding of Happiness and Well-being.* New York: Simon & Schuster.

Seligman, M. (2018) *The Optimistic Child.* London: Nicholas Brealey.

Sherrington, T. and Caviglioli, O. (2020) *Teaching Walkthrus.* Woodbridge: John Catt.

Sims, S. (2018) Four reasons instructional coaching is currently the best-evidenced form of CPD. [Online] Available at: https://samsims.education/2019/02/19/247/ (accessed 30 December 2021).

Sims, S. and Fletcher-Wood, H. (2021) Identifying the characteristics of effective teacher professional development: A critical review. *School Effectiveness and School Improvement,* 32(1): 47–63.

Sweller, J., van Merrienboer, G. and Paas, F. (1998) Cognitive architecture and instructional design. *Educational Psychology Review,* 10(3): 251–96.

Theeboom, T., Beersma, B. and Van Vianen, A. (2014) Does coaching work? A meta-analysis on the effects of coaching on individual level outcomes in an organizational context. *The Journal of Positive Psychology,* 9(1): 1–18.

Timperley, H., Kaser, L. and Halbert, J. (2014) *A Framework for Transforming Learning in Schools: Innovation and the Spiral of Inquiry.* Victoria: Centre for Strategic Education.

Timperley, H., Kaser, L. and Halbert, J. (2022) A framework for transforming learning in schools: Innovation and the spiral of inquiry. [Online] Available at: https://www.educationalleaders.govt.nz/Pedagogy-and-assessment/Evidence-based-leadership/The-spiral-of-inquiry (accessed 11 April 2022).

Tomova, L. et al. (2020) Acute social isolation evokes midbrain craving responses similar to hunger. *Nature Neuroscience,* 23: 1597–605.

Uttley, J. and Tomsett, J. (2020) *Putting Staff First.* Woodbridge: John Catt.

Watkins, M. (2013) What is organizational culture? And why should we care? [Online] Available at: https://hbr.org/2013/05/what-is-organizational-culture (accessed 8 February 2022).

White, A. (2008) *From Comfort Zone to Performance Management*. Baisy-Thy: White & MacLean Publishing.

Whitmore, J. (2017) *Coaching for Performance*. 5th edn. Boston: Nicholas Brealey Publications.

Wiliam, D. (2019) Glasgow in partnership with Tapestry's Supporting Improvement: Pedagogy and Equity Programme Award Ceremony, Glasgow.

Wilson, C. (2014) *Performance Coaching*. 2nd edn. London: Kogan Page.

Wilson, C. (2017) *Clean Language and Emergent Knowledge*. Market Harborough: Troubador Publishing.

Woodley, H. and Morrison McGill, R. (2018) *Toxic Schools: How to Avoid Them and How to Leave Them*. Woodbridge: John Catt.

World Bank (2020) Government expenditure on education. [Online] Available at: https://data.worldbank.org/indicator/SE.XPD.TOTL.GD.ZS (accessed 24 November 2021).

Index